"It's hard to put into a few words the quiet achievements of *The Unfinished Cross*. Dave Austin's writings have clarified many issues that so many of us wrestle with daily. This book serves as an invaluable road map for our lives 'from here to hereafter.'"

*Jim Peterik, founder of the musical group "Survivor"
and multi-platinum recording artist and songwriter*

"I think *The Unfinished Cross* is wonderful. I could not put it down. It is as if Dave Austin has studied our faith for the past thirty years and expressed it into words on paper."

*Michael Milligan, administrator,
Understanding Principles for Better Living Church*

"*The Unfinished Cross* is yet another beautiful verification that God's Truth is eternal and it will continue to reveal Itself to humankind as long as there are those among us who are willing to be open enough to hear it and courageous enough to speak it. Dave Austin gives us hope and new insight into this reality.

"The messengers are many, the message is the same; we live in a spiritual universe where unconditional love is always seeking divine outlets so that It may find fuller expression. Dave Austin had done a remarkable job as the messenger.

"Untouched by the opinions and dogma of people with hidden agendas, *The Unfinished Cross* is a must-read for anyone with an open mind, who desires to understand the difference between religion and spirituality. The world is ready for a fresh new look at the ancient and eternal wisdom of the greatest spiritual teacher of all time, Jesus. And, in this book, Dave Austin gives us that opportunity."

*Dr. Dennis Merritt Jones, pastor/director, Simi Valley
Religious Science Center for Positive Living*

THE
UNFINISHED CROSS

listen to the voice within

DAVE AUSTIN

HAMPTON ROADS
PUBLISHING COMPANY, INC.

for the evolving human spirit

Cover design by Marjoram Productions
Cover painting by Cathy Austin

For information write:

Hampton Roads Publishing Company, Inc.
1125 Stoney Ridge Road
Charlottesville, VA 22902

Or call: 804-296-2772
FAX: 804-296-5096
e-mail: hrpc@hrpub.com
Web site: www.hrpub.com

If you are unable to order this book from your local
bookseller, you may order directly from the publisher.
Quantity discounts for organizations are available.
Call 1-800-766-8009, toll-free.

Library of Congress Catalog Card Number: 99-91426

ISBN 1-57174-232-8

10 9 8 7 6 5 4 3 2 1

Printed on acid-free paper in the United States

Table of Contents

How many beaches must I visit,
before I feel the sand between my toes?

How many oceans must I swim
before I feel the waves splash upon my face?

How loud does God have to speak,
before I finally hear?

Acknowledgments

This book is dedicated to my wife, Cathy Austin, and Jan Adler, who together opened my eyes to what was to come; my very incredible journey, a continuing journey of searching for greater truths. A special thanks goes to my four sons, for their love and understanding while I've traveled this path of spiritual growth. Continuing thanks goes to my father, Chaplain Henry E. Austin; my mother, Deen; brother Doug; and two sisters; Ruth and Kathleen, for their love and support and their strong sense of family and Christian faith. To Alice for her love and trust, and to Ron, Wendy, Ralph, and Patti, my wonderful and loving extended family. To Ron Sobel, Ron Oberon, Todd Basse, and Pat Warfield, who all played a special role in my learning and growing experiences; those which enabled me to reach a point where I became open to writing this book. To the various authors whom I have never met, but whose books influenced me greatly and opened my eyes to new possibilities and experiences, and had a great impact on my life. Others I wish to thank are my late father-in-law, Ralph E. Shaw, and Rev. John Todd, Rev. Peter Whitlock, and Dr. Dennis Merritt Jones, as well as my first readers, Bev and Ross Bolling. Of course my biggest thanks goes to Jesus, without whom this book would never have come to fruition, but more importantly who gives me incredible strength and courage. Also, I'd like to thank my many spiritual teachers and guides who have helped throughout my life and who have been instrumental in preparing me so that I could be open and receptive enough to give these words to you.

THE
UNFINISHED CROSS

Preface

The cross is a symbol to all that Jesus showed us through dying, that we live on eternally. For, after three days, he rose again with a promise to all, that we have eternal life in the love of God, just by accepting this gracious gift of life.

The "unfinished cross" is a symbol that his teachings continue and live on, and that his work is never done. Open up your hearts and hear his messages today to build a better tomorrow. Jesus said, "I am the light." Step into the light and feel God's great love. He came to wash away your fears, for God is an all-loving Father. Know this and rejoice.

Let God's spirit complete the work of the cross within our lives.

Introduction

How I came to write with Jesus. . . .

The road which has led me to this point in my life has been quite long; long, curving, and somewhat bumpy at times. My father was a Navy chaplain, so we moved around from place to place. I have married, divorced, and married again, and am blessed to have four wonderful sons. I have changed careers numerous times and have had success in many of them. Not always success in material wealth, but nonetheless, they have all been valuable learning experiences in my life as a whole. I have been a professional athlete, traveled extensively, recorded and released a couple songs, organized and produced several large charitable events, and even pursued, with moderate success, an acting career. I have owned small businesses and have worked for others in various fields, ranging from consumer products to real estate land development. A rather varied and interesting life.

But one not without struggles. Many times, I faced one crisis or another and didn't always know where it might lead me. All of these experiences, both good and bad, were invaluable in bringing me to this exact point in my life, where I now find myself bringing this very special message to you.

Along this road of life experiences, I met an amazing woman, named Jan Adler, through my neighbor and friend, Ron. She did what is called "automatic writing," something I was not familiar with at the time. My first thought was that Ron was a nice guy, but had lost his marbles. I had been brought up with fairly traditional Christian teachings, as my father was a minister, and, as you could imagine, this concept of communicating and writing with the spirit world was a little "out there" for me.

Ron and I were in business together and he suggested sharing our booth with Jan at an upcoming trade show. I thought, why not? It might be interesting, even though I was unbelieving of what she did. As I watched other people ask her questions and she "wrote" for them, I couldn't help but notice their genuine reactions of disbelief and amazement at how she could know all that she did about their personal lives. I thought this must be fixed; these people must be planted. Surely this couldn't happen with me. So, when I had a moment, I sat down with her and started asking her some of my own questions, skeptically of course. Soon, I found myself doing the same thing that others had done all day long before me. Her answers and knowledge of my own private world were simply unbelievable. She knew very accurate things about me, including past relationships and what was going on in my life at that exact place and time. It was the most incredible experience. How did she know all this about me? Well, I came to realize that *she* didn't, but those she was "writing" with did.

Over the next several years I got to know Jan better. She became a big part of my learning experience, as I asked her more and more questions, directly leading me on my journey to being open enough to let Jesus use me to speak to you and to listen to the voice within.

I can tell you that my family became very, very nervous about this. Many times I questioned myself and wondered if I was being led astray, and actually it was my brother who helped me with this more than anything else, by saying something that I really took to heart. He said, "Ask God about it. Ask God to enter in to help see if this is a part of him." I took his advice and it helped me immensely by relieving my fears. My concern was that I might be going down a path that was dark and foolish, one that was actually turning away from God. I asked God to be a part of it, and this opened me up and allowed me to see things that I was not able to see before.

Back then I never dreamed that I would one day begin to write myself. However, after getting to know Jan and having her write for me over several years, I found myself compelled to pick up a pen and paper and write during an overseas flight to Germany. It didn't really seem like anything at the time, it was merely thoughts coming, and in turn I was just writing them down. Now, in business, if I was ever going to write a letter or memo, even if it was going to be only one paragraph, I would struggle for hours because I would agonize over each word. But during this experience, I was filled with words. I couldn't write fast enough to keep up with them. I was flooded with words and it went on for page after page, which was very unique for me.

After awhile I stopped and was too tired to read what was there, so it wasn't until later that I actually read the words and found how remarkable they were. During that same trip, I awoke during the night and was compelled again to write. I couldn't really comprehend what was going on, but grabbed the paper and pen, and for several hours wrote again. Once finished, I put the writing aside and went back to sleep. It wasn't until the trip home that I pulled it out to read. It almost felt as if it had been a dream, even though I knew I had gotten up and done it, but I couldn't remember what I had written. Then I read the words and I was astonished.

Upon returning home, I shared these writings with my wife and she was truly amazed. I then called Jan, but was almost too embarrassed, since I didn't want her to think that I now thought I could "write" just like her. When she heard the words, she was surprised at how clear the messages had come through for me. Encouraged, I continued to write, but was very reluctant for the first few years. I wouldn't share this experience with many others, and there were times I'd say I wasn't going to continue with it either. It was just too difficult for me to completely understand what was taking place. My wife, however, gently pushed and encouraged me, and the words continued to flow. Now, I pass them on in this book.

Since these writings began, I've had many different guides or teachers who, having lived on this earth before, now "write" through me to pass along messages. During one of these writings, Jesus said, *"Hello, I am here."* Immediately I stopped and my first thought was, oh my God, what has this become? Have I stepped over the line and gone off the deep end? Have I completely lost it? How can Jesus be talking to me?

It's interesting that I would say "how could Jesus be talking to me," when the Christian belief is that Jesus talks to us each and every day. Jesus indeed talks to us in the Scriptures. Then why do we accept the fact that God could talk directly to those living 2,000 years ago and prior to that, and yet it is hard to comprehend that he could continue doing so today, with us? Doesn't he have the ability to do this anymore? Did God just decide to stop creating? Why are we more comfortable with God speaking with those who lived so long ago?

These are the questions that came to mind when I began, ever so slowly at first, to write with Jesus. But I must admit, I felt unworthy. Have you heard that one before? It seems everyone who was ever a part of Jesus' life, or whom God spoke to, as you read in history and in the Bible, always replied, "I'm not worthy." Now I personally know that feeling. So I shared the writing only with my wife, not knowing exactly where it was going. Mostly it was just helping me live my own personal life with my family. And what a huge difference it made in my life. It was unbelievable the impact it had on, one, my happiness, and two, knowing what I truly wanted, rather than just living day-to-day in what I now call "unconscious living."

Writing with Jesus has become as comfortable as talking with one of my dearest friends. I find myself living more aware of God's love, and I continually ask for him to be a part of all my decisions and actions. I am thankful for this relationship with Jesus, and for the open nature it has developed into. It's amazing how the beauty of the natural surroundings seems to radiate with a new intensity, and how I experience more love for my wife and family. I find life more enjoyable and an incredible experience, one that I hope everyone can have. It doesn't mean that we won't have ups and downs in this physical life. But when you know God is a part of *all* of it, and those ups and downs are just a part of us experiencing life in this physical form, you begin to live life differently. It is God experiencing life in a physical form through us, giving us all individual souls and individual choices and free will. Even while knowing this, I still have my moments when I slip completely away into "unconscious living"; but overall I've been able to become incredibly positive about most things.

One day I came across a little shop called Angels Among Us. It looked interesting and I was compelled to go in and look around. I am now more willing to act on these thoughts or hunches, to see where they might lead me and what I might learn or encounter from them. In other words, I have become open to let go and follow my instincts, rather than closing myself off from them. I am thankful to God for this, and for reading one book in particular that opened my eyes to this way of thinking.

I walked into the shop and looked around asking myself, what is the reason for being here? What is going to inspire me? I looked through several books, saw one in particular that looked interesting, and asked the shop owner what she thought of the book. She said it was good, but suggested I read a very fascinating book called *Conversations with God*. I questioned, "*Conversations with God*"? After listening to her summary of the book, I thought, here is another person who is basically doing inspired writing, but who is "writing" with God. I then knew immediately why I was there and that this was a book I just had to read.

I bought *Conversations with God* and started reading it, but then my wife snatched it, read it, and was completely captured by it. After she was done, she immediately went out and bought the next book in its three-part series, along with the taped version of the first book. Actually, this is how I got to know what was written in the first book: I listened. It was both very inspiring and amazing. Here I'd been writing with Jesus for several years and this gentleman claimed to be writing with God. It made me a little more comfortable that there was another person who was either just as crazy as I, or indeed, we were both receiving very important messages through divine means, affirming that this could really be happening. When I say "could really be happening," that's the toughest part. It's so easy to believe in things that happened 2,000 years ago or something that is far removed from us. But when it happens right now, right in front of us, it's hard to comprehend that it could really be taking place.

Well, I listened to the tapes, and found that many of the things that I was discovering in my own writings were coming out in his writings; it made sense of things that for a long time I had problems with within my own religion, and brought together answers to certain parts of the Bible that I found were contradictory at times. It was remarkable that this book was so in sync with what both my wife and I had grown to know and believe through my writings, through Jan's writings, and through our own personal learning experiences together.

The day I picked up *Conversations with God*, I went on to have a talk with the shop owner and shared with her that I, too, was "writing" some. I did this since I felt she had an open mind and wouldn't think I was absolutely crazy (even though I wasn't brave enough to tell her *who* I was writing with). Out of the blue, she said, "You really should write a book." I looked at her and said skeptically, "Yeah right." Well, one thing lead to another and I got "pushed" again when Jesus asked me to read and get to know the Scriptures.

As mentioned before, I was brought up on traditional Christian teachings, and even though I didn't completely understand what I believed in, I knew basically that I believed in Jesus Christ and God, and in doing good for others. I also had a great deal of skepticism for anything that deviated from what I was told the Bible said. Since I never really studied the Bible myself, nor understood how to let the Bible inspire me, I always accepted what others *said* it meant. What bothered me, though, was that often what one person said it meant contradicted what another said about the very same words.

The Bible is an amazing book. It's a book that is part of our experience with Christ and God. It is a book that can enable us to be inspired, just as it was originally written, through inspirations to those that authored it. When you read the Bible, ask God to inspire you to understand some of its meanings. Many out there preach that it is so simple, that it's black and white. But the Bible isn't. If it's so black and white, why do many people interpret it and use it in so many different ways?

If you choose to read and learn the Bible, open yourself up to asking God to be a part of your experience with it. Ask him to be in your reading of it, in that which it teaches you, and in your acceptance of what the meaning of living it is. Then listen to your heart and know its messages.

As I've said, the Bible is an amazing book; one that was written so many years ago, is now in so many different languages, and still has absolute meaning in millions of people's lives. There is no book ever written before or after the Bible that has had this same impact. Yet, over time there have been various translations and different words used, ones that have had different meanings during different time periods. I feel this is why Jesus was now asking me to read the Bible, and to let him "write" through me, in today's language, the messages he came and preached back then.

So, I began doing that. In the past when I attempted to read the Bible, I could never get very far. I found it too confusing. I found it hard to read. I would find myself daydreaming, and before I'd even know it, I'd be nodding off to sleep. Then I would feel guilty. I would say to myself, why can't I be inspired, why can't I read this book and understand it? I believe I am not alone in this thinking. However, through this experience of writing with Jesus, I now have been able to be "inspired" with the words of the Bible, and it has brought forth a whole new meaning in my life.

For the first time, the words of the Bible were interesting and kept me enthralled. I then began "writing" with Jesus and it became another incredible experience. The Bible, which had been so difficult for me to read, suddenly became very open and meaningful. I found a direct relationship between what I had written with Jesus, and the messages that were contained in *Conversations with God*. Previously I thought the two writings didn't necessarily go together. Now I know, through this experience, that they do.

When people read this, they may accuse me of blasphemy and say that I'm using Christ's name for my own needs. But I feel the Bible can be inspirational today if you'll read it and have your own *personal* experience with God. He'll talk to you. I've personally learned this in my life. Be open to really believing that. Many people say they believe, that they believe in the miracles that were written in the Bible, but they can't seem to trust and believe completely enough that these things can happen to them today. Miracles can happen and they do. Angels *are* among us. They are here to give us help and guidance. Just listen and be open to hearing their messages.

What's more, through God's love, we can "heal" ourselves. Now that's an amazing thing. We can heal ourselves. I have had many experiences which show me that, yes, absolutely we can. It makes no sense at all to believe that God was able to do these things years ago, but then accept that he can't do it now. Why not now? Why not today? Why not through us? Jesus didn't have special magic. He was simply in tune with God and let him be a part of everything. And if we do this, we are capable of "moving mountains," each and every one of us. Jesus found it to be much easier because he knew exactly who he was, where he was going, and where he was from. We, however, tend to get lost. It's tougher for us to find our way. We need to listen. We need to let him help us in our lives today. Listen and trust. You will hear.

As I was first writing this book, I found that I had so many questions. Why am I doing this, and what *am* I doing? Once this book is published, people might think I am absolutely crazy. A few years back I was one who would have said, "This guy's a little off the beaten track." It is difficult for me to put this out there for all to see, just as it was difficult when I began to write down these inspirations coming through to me. I was amazed then, and continue to be amazed. Yes, there are still times that I think, what will my friends say? They know nothing of this, and how will they react to me when they know? Will they feel that I believe I have a special relationship with Jesus? It is true that I do, but it is a relationship that anyone can have if they are willing to and choose to.

Anybody can have this one-on-one relationship, even though it's taken years for me to open up to it. Perhaps these words will help you to open up too. Each of us has been given free will to do whatever we'd like, and if we choose to live and make choices out of love, rather than fear and anger, we can experience a life here that can truly be "heaven on earth." It is my sincere desire that, through these words, you are able to make choices out of love and to experience all that love has to offer you in this life. That's my prayer for today and tomorrow. It is for you to have a life knowing that God is a part of everything, and that we are here to experience, physically, all the love and glory of God.

This has brought every aspect of my life to a much brighter level. As I have already mentioned, the love for my family is stronger, and my experiences in general are felt with greater intensity. If your heart is open and you feel God's presence, you will make life choices that can bring great joy. It's never too late to create and to keep on creating. God is creating every day. We make free choices in this life, and in doing so, we have, at times, absolutely torn and ripped apart the beauty that God has created. But it is not too late for us, as human beings, to use the power of thoughts and actions to help repair the damage that has been done. If you find yourself doing something that you are not happy with, re-create it at that very moment and create new thoughts and create new actions.

There was another example of the "pushes" which led me to the writing of this book. My son, who goes to a private Christian school, had an assignment to select a portion of the Scriptures and explain what it meant to him. The following are the selections he chose from Proverbs 3 NIV (New International Version):

> 3 Let love and faithfulness never leave you;
> bind them around your neck,
> write them on the tablet of your heart.

4   Then you will win favor and a good name
    in the sight of God and man.
7   Do not be wise in your own eyes;
    fear the Lord and shun evil.
8   This will bring health to your body
    and nourishment to your bones.
11 My son, do not despise the Lord's
    discipline and do not resent his rebuke.
12 Because the Lord disciplines those he loves
    as a father the son he delights in.

He asked my wife and me what we thought it meant. But, instead of giving him our opinions, and since I was writing with Jesus at that time, we decided to ask Jesus directly. His words in reply were again both amazing and, at the same time, comforting (refer to chapter 15, page 119 for related dialogue):

Jesus is here. Go ahead.

Love will bring you joy.
See love in all things.

Be wise in your own eyes.
Never fear the Lord.
Embrace the Lord and all that is good.

Face evil, do not fear evil.
The light of the love of God will get you through
every experience.

You will experience all. God has created all.
If you experience sorrow or pain,
know that God is in all things and take heart in
this knowledge.

If you truly believe that God inspired the Bible, then you must believe that people today can be inspired directly by God; unless, of course, you feel that God quit working 2,000 years ago. I don't know if you would call it "the straw that broke the camel's back," but after we had this experience with my son's school assignment, I said, "Okay, Jesus, I'm listening. I will write with you, and hear the Scriptures through you and through my experiences with you."

Well, I just happened to open the Bible to 1 John, so I wrote on it with Jesus. When I was finished with 1 John, I was told to go back and write on the Book of Matthew. I was also told that this is exactly how the Bible was written so very long ago: through inspirations from God. Please realize, this was, and is, a very hard thing for me to comprehend. I was writing inspirations down, just as the authors had written that which became part of the Bible. However, by this time I was able to just let go and say, "God lead me and I will follow your direction."

As you read through this book, you might find yourself questioning whether these messages are directly from Jesus, or if they are just a part of the author's own imagination. Regardless of their origin, step back and decide for yourself: do the words help you to live your life differently and in a more positive direction? Are you happier in general, and do you enjoy life more living these principles? Take from this book what you can. Don't worry if you aren't sure about this or that, or find it hard to accept all of it as your own truth. As you would do with a school assignment, if you come to an area that you have problems with, an area that you may struggle with, one that you might not necessarily agree with, skip ahead to see what you can discover in the next part. After you have finished, go back and try reading those difficult areas again. Maybe this time when you hear these words, they might affect you differently; and then again, maybe they won't. This is your life. Do with it what you choose, and make your own decisions by listening to the voice within.

What I sincerely hope is that you receive from these writings something positive, something that you can use while going forward in your everyday life, something that makes your life here on earth a better one—both for yourself in your own journey, and for those you meet along the way. I truly believe that we are here to work together by helping each other, and most importantly, by loving one another. May you be successful in this journey, and may you find love and happiness along the way.

chapter 1

Inspirations

The process in which I began this ongoing dialogue fell into a pattern where I would sit down, close my eyes, and quiet my mind. I would ask Jesus to come through to my pen with clarity, and that the messages would be directly from him. After a few moments, I would write down, "Jesus is here. Go ahead," and the thoughts would come flowing through me and the dialogue would begin. Throughout the book, you will see this statement, "Jesus is here. Go ahead," indicating that the messages following are directly from him.

Jesus is here. Go ahead.

Q. Why are you passing these messages on, and why through me?

Why not through you? You have become open to listening to your inner self. Is this message not important for all to hear? This message is everywhere, but most refuse to hear it. Many are beginning to open up and listen. This is why you find these same messages in other books as well. The more this message is brought forward, the more it breaks down the barriers and more people will open up and start hearing it.

Look at your own journey and what transpired in your life to bring you to this point of acceptance and openness. I was bringing this message before, but you were not aware. This message is everywhere for all to grab hold of. A parable of this would be: You walk into a room and there is a very intriguing picture on the wall. You glance at it, but other objects in the room take your attention away. Later, someone asks you about the picture and you don't recall it, or if you do recall it, you can't remember it in detail.

The face of God is everywhere, but you have to be aware or you don't see or feel this presence. God is within all of you and you are all a part of God.

Words don't do justice in explaining who God is. Think of a great body of water, then take a drop of this water out. See yourself as this drop of water. You are a part of the greater body of water, and that body of water is a part of you. So are you a part of God? Yes. But, are you all God is? No. You can take a drop of water out of the greater body of water and it becomes an individual drop; it is made up of the whole body of water, but it is not all of the water. You can put the drop of water back into the larger body of water, and it again becomes part of the whole.

You need not think of God as a man or a

woman, for he has no gender. I use the word "he" for simplicity. God is everything. God is all there is. God is within all, and all is a part of God.

Q. How do we begin? Shall I continue to just write the words as they come?

Yes, this is how the Bible was written; through inspirations from God.

People have a hard time believing that something that happened 2,000 years ago can happen today. But it is important to expand on the Bible in today's language to help tie it all together. This can be a guide to understanding what was communicated in the Bible so long ago.

This book is very important if you want to help enlighten the world. You are tuned in, and we are willing and able, as always, to communicate. The Bible needs to be adapted to today's language. When it was first inspired, the human physical forms had different needs and yearnings.

Q. Can I ask you specific questions I have with the Bible?

Yes, ask me about the Bible. I will bring you today the messages that I preached, void of any interpretations that have developed over time.

Q. Do I personally need to read the Bible to write on this with you?

Absolutely. It can't be a one-sided conversation. You need to know what we are talking about to be able to ask questions and enlighten today's meanings into the words.

chapter 2

Where Are You Now?

When I turned in what I thought was the final manuscript to the publisher, the editor came back with a question for Jesus: Where is he now? The following is his reply:

Jesus is here. Go ahead.

Q. Where are you now?

I am everywhere. This is the hardest concept to grasp, because when you are in physical form, you are limited to where you are at that exact moment. To go someplace else, you either need to walk, run, or use some form of transportation to get there. In the spiritual world, you can be everywhere. No mode of transportation is needed and there are no time limitations. This is like answering the question, how far is infinity? Human minds have this need to know limits. That is why individual limitations are different. God has given every individual this wonderful gift of "free choice," so each of you can decide your own limits. Your limitations are based on your own established limits, not God's limits. For God has created a perfect world and has no limits.

Life is evolving every moment of every day, and your individual free will, combined with the free will of those who share this physical life around you, create and continue the evolutionary process. So it is your belief system that tells you what you are. If you tell yourself you can only do this or that, then that is all you will be able to do. When I healed, it was because I completely believed in the healing power that God has created within all of us, and I combined this with the recipient's faith or belief. I am quoted in the Bible for something I said many times over: "It is done unto you as you believe." In this physical world, many have to see physical proof for them to believe. This does not mean that something doesn't exist because you can't see it physically; it just means that those who believe in God and believe in faith can feel the unseen become a part of them.

So who is God? God is everything and everywhere. Don't try to put limitations on who God is. Know that you are a part of God, as are those around you. So are doctors important in this physical world? Absolutely. Even though you all have the power to heal, God is also working through doctors. To say you never need a doctor would be limiting who God is and what he is a part of. Is God a part of the bad in the world? Absolutely. God is all there is. But, God does not "will" destruction or hate. Many are quick to say, "Well it must be 'God's will'." Take responsibility for your life and make God a part of everything you do. He already is, but your awareness of this fact will help you make good choices in your life and comprehend God's great abundance.

In the afterlife, you can be anywhere and everywhere. You can create any setting you want. If you believe in a hell and feel this is where you belong, you can create this. If you believe in a heaven with pearly gates, you can create this also. God has created all right here on earth. Go to the mountains or deserts; go to the areas where it is easiest for you to feel one with God. Then bring that experience back with you, so you can feel that oneness wherever you are. In the spiritual world, you can create the greatest meadow, or the most beautiful lake. When you know of your oneness with God, all is possible.

chapter 3

Genesis

Although I haven't spent time writing with
Jesus on all the different books of the Old
Testament, I wanted to spend some time with him
on Genesis, the first book of the Bible. What
came through to me shed light on how, even
when we hear the voice of God within us, we are
affected by our own physical experiences at that
moment in time. I was once told by a seminary
student that he does not have his wife wear a head
cover in church, as is directed by Paul in 1
Corinthians 11:5-6, due to the fact that one must
understand what was going on in the context of
that time period to fully understand the words
written there. I pointed out that he was suggest-
ing that this meant Paul was influenced by his
own physical conditions and knowledge of the
world at that time, and that his written words
were then a product of that personal knowledge
of the world. The student seemed to be caught in

a contradiction at this point, because moments earlier he had spoken so passionately about how wrong, and forbidden, it was to change even one word of the Bible.

If we are to take it so literally, then shouldn't women still be wearing head coverings? If it had such importance to mankind that it was included in this great book, then why are we not expected to follow it word-for-word? I believe, and what I feel this student was trying to get across to me was, that we must take a look at what the traditions and culture of that time period dictated, and apply the words of the Bible to our own personal lives based on the traditions and culture of today's world. I also believe that we must take into consideration what influences the writer of these words had within his own life. I agree that the Bible was created through God's inspirations, but it was written by men, and translated into different languages over thousands of years by other men, to the best of their abilities. The following is Jesus' reply to me when I questioned him on the meanings of Genesis.

Jesus is here. Go ahead.

This message was delivered to a human in the physical world who felt the world was flat. When you write, you cannot help but bring your own viewpoint into this writing. Just as when you write with me, your knowledge of universal things plays a role in the final words that are on this paper. You hear the message the way you need to hear it. Just like in *Conversations with God*, Neale Donald Walsch heard his message through years of frustration with the church and religion, but his exposure was much different from your experience. That is why you will write words that have a different feeling to them; it is the same basic message, but your life will influence the words just as his experiences did. This is not bad or good; it is just so. Scriptures are not wrong; they are just outdated and misinterpreted in some instances.

The basic message in Genesis is that God created the earth and the physical world as you know it. He created all of this to experience his thoughts through you and all of mankind. God wants to pass on unconditional love, and experience unconditional love. Love is a big part of life because it is the greatest feeling man can experience and share with others. This does not mean he cannot handle evil and conditional love. To experience all, he must let human existence have free will. Without this free will, he would be unable to experience all things, just as human souls would be limited in their experiences. Why create, if you can only create exact good? You must be free to experience all, and part of experiencing all is the consequences that come from doing all.

If a man (or woman) chooses to kill another human being, then the consequences are to live with that knowledge and feeling—either by living in a controlled jail experience or by losing your life on earth for that life experience; or, when no one knows, and you are free, but you are never really free. Whether the courts convict a person or not, they can live "hell on earth," when it is possible to live "heaven on earth."

Many of you (most of you) are waiting for the afterlife to start living in God's "heaven." It is simply too hard for you to have enough faith in the message of God—that heaven and pure love can be obtained in this existence. When your father-in-law, Ralph, and Jan left this physical form, they looked back and wondered why they didn't get it completely while they were here, when in fact the message after passing on seems so simple. Your father, Hank, knew this, and even though he got lost in many ways through human weaknesses, he ultimately knew and had complete faith.

chapter 4

1 John 1-5

My approach to writing on 1 John was to read the Bible verse-by-verse, then ask Jesus to explain what it meant. He explained each verse in his own words. Although you won't see the verses repeated, it goes along in order as it is presented in the Bible and gives chapter and verse. You might find it helpful to read this chapter while at the same time referencing what is written in the Bible.

Jesus is here. Go ahead.

1 John 1

Yes, the message is the same I bring to you now. You all have strayed from whom you want to be, and this is described as sin. Yes, you have all sinned, but this is just experiencing life. When you go through life unconsciously and bring darkness or conditioned habits into it, you are not fulfilling who you are and want to be. Sin is darkness. God is light. Create your actions from this knowledge, and feel the joy this brings to you and to those you come in contact with.

1 John 2

There is no God's wrath. This is a missed message of interpretation, for God loves unconditionally and has no wrath. What I did was bring the light of the world up close and personal so those around me could experience it fully, and, by doing so, open up to experience the full joy of life and walk away from the darkness of unconscious living—presented here as "washing away your sins."

Sin is not the right word; fooling yourselves is a better word here. Fooling yourselves and not opening up to my teachings so you can experience life more fully and experience who you want to be. You cannot become who you truly want to be without opening up and experiencing life as I have taught. When you do this, your life is enriched and full of the joy this brings. This wording makes it look like a command; what should be heard is that if you live as I did, your life will be more fulfilled.

There is no power over those who live in this knowledge of God's warmth and love. "Satan," or darkness, or lack of acceptance of this love, brings on an existence in darkness. When you love one another, the darkness in your lives disappears, and the new light of life from me shines in.

Words so pure as these need nothing more:

The Living Bible
1 John 2:9-11

9 Anyone who says he is walking in the light of Christ, but dislikes his fellow man, is still in darkness.

10 But whoever loves his fellow man is 'walking in the light' and can see his way without stumbling around in darkness and sin.

11 For he who dislikes his brother is wandering in spiritual darkness and doesn't know where he is going, for the darkness has made him blind so that he cannot see the way.

"Satan" is another word for a soul lost in darkness.

Wealth is wonderful. Sex is wonderful. The true meaning here is: If you let these be your god and they control you, then you live in darkness and can't fully enjoy the true essence of life and love. Money and material things without love in your heart are meaningless. Sex without love in your heart is meaningless.

Those who speak out against me are still with us and a part of us. These people, or souls, are just in darkness; that is all. Let your bright light lead them back into the light. Do not condemn them; open your hearts to them so they can feel the warmth of love and can be brought back into the light.

By seeing how I lived, it is easier to experience all of God's love. God loves everyone, even the non-believers. The non-believers are not experiencing the joy of this love because they are closed to it, as they are lost in darkness.

It is not a matter of doing right or wrong in God's eyes, because he loves unconditionally. It is only a matter of you being able to experience this love in its fullest form. When you open yourself to this love, you experience "heaven on earth" in all experiences.

1 John 3

God is experiencing life through you—each and every one of you. Yes, you are all his children and creation. You will try to keep remembering who you are and experiencing your love of life, just as I lived.

Every man, woman, and all of creation are his and always will be. If you are in darkness, you can't fully experience God's love and the beauty of it all. I came here to show you the light and the way to fully-conscious living, rather than living in darkness and not being open to all of God's experiences that he has presented to each of you.

You are all born into God's family. I came to teach and enlighten you, to open each of you to conscious living, and to feel the power of God's love. By living your life in this love and knowledge, it helps you to become who you want to be, and helps you to experience life in its fullest intent. Those who don't, don't. They are not cast away by God, but they live in darkness and don't experience the true love of God, which is available for all to feel and experience.

I came to bring the light of God's love to each and every one of you, and to bring those who are in darkness into the light. Those who step out of the darkness and into the light will feel as though they have been born again, and they will continue to seek knowledge and remember who they are. All are children of God. With this knowledge, every aspect of life is quite different and more fulfilling.

"All are in God's family."

Even those in darkness. Those who experienced the light and love of God love their brother and sister and all, and, in this love, live a joyous life. Those who live in darkness and fear don't have this experience. That is all. You can see those who radiate love and those who don't. Those who radiate love and compassion are extremely enjoyable to be around. Those who don't, aren't.

If we are like Cain, we hate ourselves because we are not who we want to be. Fear creates hate. Love creates peace.

Each and every one of you has eternal life. Some live in the knowledge and the light, and others are in darkness without this knowledge. Those who live with hate carry with them great amounts of fear. Feeling God's love fully washes away these fears.

Actions speak louder than words. Do unto others as you would have done unto you. Show your love and compassion in your everyday living, and in the things that you do. Don't just talk about caring for others; live it in your actions and your decisions.

If we know who we are and show this in our actions, we feel better about ourselves and our relationship with God. But if you stray, this does not mean that God turns his back on you, for he will never do this. It is for you to decide to turn around and face him and feel his everlasting love.

1 John 4

To know if a message is from God, simply ask God, and feel his answer deep within you. There are many who will give false meanings to God's word to better their physical existence here on earth. They live in darkness to God's true love. So simply talk with God, open yourself to his answers, and always ask God to open your eyes to the fact that he is within all things and experiences.

Those who get caught up in this physical existence and live for rewards that are strictly for the present, with no thoughts of tomorrow and eternal existence, live only for momentary gladness. Those who live with God's love deep within their hearts shall see beauty and experience greater pleasure than those who seek worldly possessions and live in darkness of God's love. Is this a message from God? Just ask yourself: Does this message help you to live with God's love in your heart, or does it take you into darkness, away from his warmth and love?

Choose to live and have your actions initiated from love. You will feel the warmth of God's love by being open to it and living it every day in all your actions.

God sent me into the world to enlighten those who were wasting away in darkness, growing further and further away from knowing the true meaning of God's love. Many Scriptures have said I came to wash away God's anger against your sins. God is never angry at you; he gave you free will to choose who you are and want to be. But one can get lost in darkness living away from the knowledge of God's love and the strength and growth it brings to everyone every day. I came to be the light and bring you this truth of God's eternal love.

Knowing that God is love, and choosing to live with this knowledge in your heart, and choosing actions with this love deep within you will bring great joy. Don't be ashamed if you have let your life slip away from this knowledge of God's love. But open up to it, and feel the strength and joy it brings you to face God and embrace him with this love.

Don't fear God, for his love is always with you, even if you have slipped into darkness. Take the warmth of his love and pass it on to all those around you. For if you truly feel the power and warmth of God's love, it is easy to pass this on to all those with whom you come in contact, and you will feel the joy this brings to you and to those who embrace your love and take it in.

1 John 5

All creatures and all things are from God, and you are all his children.

I came and taught that by feeling God's love and passing this love on in each and every choice you make, you will live in the warmth of his light. The more you share and live this message, the more you will wash away the darkness and live with the joy of knowing God's love.

I am the son of God, but all of you are children of God.

I came to bring this message to all. If you believe in me and believe in yourself as children and a part of God, this knowledge and acceptance will bring you eternal life in the light and warmth of God's love. Without this you cannot experience God's love, and you turn to darkness. It is easy to live eternally in God's love; just accept it, and feel it within your soul. Communicate with God daily and he will communicate with you. Ask and listen and make him a part of each and every aspect of your life. Do this and you will have peace in the fact that you live eternally in his love.

If you experience others around you who live in darkness of God's love, don't condemn them. Pray for them so they can see the light and feel the joy of God's love. God never turns his back on anyone, and he is always there. "Satan" has no power over those who live in this knowledge of God's warmth and love.

As I've said before, "Satan," or darkness, or lack of acceptance of this love, brings on existence in darkness.

chapter 5

Interlude

While living in this physical world, it is very easy to get sidetracked and to let our present needs take priority. These writings with Jesus got put off for a while, as I devoted my time to the "daily grind." One day, my wife and I got into a long discussion about something, which prompted me to pick up a pen and writing pad for the first time in a long while. She then pointed out to me that I needed to take the time to continue my writings, and that I had to have faith that we would be fine. She went on to say that no monetary or physical needs were more important than these writings. Everything would take care of itself if we had complete faith and trust. It might mean we would have to give up our home or our cars, but we would ultimately have something of more value: We would have the opportunity to share love and knowledge with others.

Jesus is here. Go ahead.

It's about time you and Cathy got back into this kind of discussion.

Yes, this is what you have to do. You have let fear guide you right now. Put out love and let it take over your life again. Everything works when handled in this way. Don't beat yourself up. You are human, living a physical life with real physical desires and monetary needs that get in the way. But this is all part of the learning process, and you gain in every experience.

The Book of Matthew is a complete account of my life when I was here, living in the physical world, so let's continue there. Read it again, and as you do, we will then write on it together.

chapter 6

The Book of Matthew 1-28

In contrast to the manner in which I approached the writings in 1 John, I did not go verse by verse with the Book of Matthew. I read each chapter in its entirety and then allowed my pen to take flight with the words that flowed thereafter.

Jesus is here. Go ahead.

Matthew 1

This gives my line of heritage, starting with King David down to Mary and Joseph. God chose to bring me into the world with Mary as a virgin to give validity to what was about to take place in Joseph and Mary's life. As you find it difficult to accept that I am speaking to you today, you must know how difficult it was for Mary and Joseph to accept the fact that God had chosen them to bear me into this world. The fact that Mary remained a virgin until my birth helped Mary through times of doubt, and Joseph's dream gave validity to him in times of doubt.

It is easy for those to accept something that happened far in the past because they don't have to face straight up to it in their own living experience. If you think of how it would affect you today to know you are bearing a child into this world for God to enlighten the world, you have the ability to imagine what Joseph and Mary had to go through. David, you have fought against writing this book because of your own self-doubt in the fact that you were chosen to bring this message into print today, in this world.

Joseph and Mary struggled with all this, just as you do today. But they let their faith lead them and prayed to God to be a part of all things. With this, they gained the strength to accept the fact that they were bringing this special child into the world. Joseph, at first, was furious and broken-hearted that Mary was pregnant, for he knew he had not made love to her. Then an angel, or messenger, appeared to him in a dream and told Joseph that his son was from God and that Mary was still a virgin. This son would be named Jesus and would bring the word of their Father, God, into the world. Joseph married Mary and, with strong faith, believed and brought me into the world and raised me with a loving, guiding hand, as Mary did also.

Matthew 2

I was born in Bethlehem. God presented a bright star above Bethlehem as a sign of my birth. King Herod was told of my birth and sought to kill me, for his fear ruled his actions and he saw me as a threat to his kingdom. An angel appeared to Joseph and told him of this, so Joseph and Mary brought me to Egypt until the death of King Herod. We then moved back to Israel and lived in Nazareth. I lived and learned my father's trade of a carpenter.

Matthew 3

John the Baptist was a strong preacher, and he captured the attention of all those who would listen. He baptized those who wanted to feel the cleansing and warmth of God's love. He asked those who came to be baptized to open their hearts and minds to God's love and to ask God to be a part of every aspect of their lives. With this knowledge of God's presence in all things, they saw life through new eyes; and this warmth and love of God, that they now acknowledged, brought new meaning to their lives.

When I was baptized by John, I felt God's great presence like I had never felt it before on this earth. I knew then that it was time for me to go out and bring God's message to the world. I knew without a doubt that God had brought me into this world to bring those out of darkness and from a lack of knowledge to the true meaning of living in God's loving arms.

We all have free choices to experience all things, but acting and living in the knowledge of God's love brings with it new meaning to your life. It creates choices in your actions that bring forth greater joy and fulfillment, greater than anything you can possibly experience without this knowledge. When you are truly at one with this knowledge, God's natural beauties are so much more beautiful and meaningful in your life. Even in hardship, you can endure anything if you keep God's love strong in your heart.

Matthew 4

Living in human flesh had all the same temptations for me that you face each day, and I, too, had to make decisions on my own. But by knowing who God was and asking daily for his guidance, I made my choices to help me become who I truly wanted to be. Those who ask daily for God's guidance will receive it fully. Take time out each and every day to get grounded in this knowledge of God's existence and love. You will see how differently you live this life and how much greater and fulfilling your life will become. There is such great joy in making decisions out of love for yourself and for those you come in contact with. When your decisions are made from fear (be it fear from not being this or that, fear that you won't have all the toys in the world that you want, fear that someone else is getting what you deserve), then you will experience the consequences that this brings, and the anger that blocks you from the joys this life can fully bring.

I was known for my healing powers. You all have these powers within. It's just fully believing and asking God to bring his love through you to heal whatever is ailing someone. Also, God created nature. There is a great giving and taking if you let the beauty of nature's energy pass through you. I would ask God to fill my hands with his love and have those I was touching feel the strength of this love pass through to them, and as their blood circulated through their bodies, to feel the cleansing and the healing power it would bring them. I would also draw upon the trees and grass and my natural surroundings, for a great deal of energy radiates from these living, God-created things. As I drew from this energy, the trees and plants would feel my love, and my energy would also pass through them, and they would appear more beautiful than I had ever known. They would take on a glow and brightness, and I would feel the power of their living form pass through me to help heal whatever was ailing the person I was with.

You all have this capability; it is just a simple matter of being aware of it and asking. It is a beautiful thing, because it is giving and taking at the same time. You are bringing stronger life to God's universe, and in return this natural universe is sending energy through you that is so very healing.

If someone is not being healed when you feel you have tapped into this powerful gift from God, don't be discouraged and give up. Continue on a daily basis, and ask God to be with you every step of the way. Then, no matter what physically happens, you will know that God's love has been passed through you. And if, for example, someone passes on from this physical existence, it does not mean that you didn't heal this soul; you did, only in a way that is hard for you to understand, unless you fully believe in eternal life in many forms with God.

As I lived and preached, I gathered others to follow me to teach this love of God and to bring his light into the darkness of those who did not yet experience all the great warmth of love that he has to offer—to show how this knowledge and experience could change lives.

It is so easy to get caught up in everyday living experiences and to live by immediate needs and wants that are a part of this physical living experience. Even those with the greatest intentions fall into habits that bring them to forget what life can be when they let God be a part of all things. He is a part of all things; it is just a matter of knowing this that will bring about actions and choices that will bring you far greater joy and satisfaction. Don't wait to die from this physical existence that God has given you to experience heaven. Experience it now, each and every day.

Matthew 5

God is love. Preach this knowledge to those who appear both weak or strong. You can handle any persecution from others you experience here in this physical existence just with the simple knowledge that you know and experience God's love each and every day. Don't hate those who persecute you, for they are in darkness of this knowledge. Be a light that might bring them to this knowledge also. Don't strive to be better than those around, just strive to be knowledgeable of God's love, and let this affect your decisions daily.

Matthew speaks passionately in this book because of his own guilt—because of his own lust and desires. I say don't let this guilt rule your life and actions; simply bring God's love into all things and into the choices you make. God will never turn his back on you. Don't try to do good deeds because of your fear of God's wrath. Do good deeds because it fills you with great joy and brings your life to its fullest form. Don't fight fear and guilt. When you feel it coming, just acknowledge it, and it will not control your actions.

Matthew 6

Prayer, our communication with God, is important each and every day if you are striving to live each and every moment in God's love and grace. Communicate and talk to God daily, constantly. This does not mean go out to show others how you talk to God and only pray publicly, but to communicate with God privately and develop your own special relationship with God. By doing this daily, you let him become more a part of your life. And the feeling of his love wrapped around will help you take each moment this life brings you and see it through loving, caring eyes. Your reactions will then be generated out of this love, rather than fear. If you let fear guide you, you will move further from God's love and your actions will be generated by this fear. You can't have both, because if you bring God into all things and communicate with him as your closest friend, then the fear will dissipate and all is manageable through love.

God has provided everything you need to survive in this life. Don't fear that you will not have food enough for tomorrow, just ask God to bring forth answers to all situations, and listen and be conscious of all that is around you. When you are looking for riches, know that there is no greater wealth than the feeling of God's love. You can have all the money in the world, but nothing compares to the knowledge and strength you feel when living in God's love. You could have the greatest wealth and build great castles, but there is no beauty more beautiful than God's given natural surroundings. And there is no greater joy than loving those around you. Deep, pure love brings a comfort that no monetary wealth could ever bring. There is no beauty greater than the natural surroundings that God has created.

God has given you free will and choice for you to experience all things. You have a choice to see things through loving and caring eyes, or not. But, by seeing clearly through your own eyes with a pure heart, you will truly see and feel the beauty of this life which God has created. This does not mean to cast your eyes away from the destruction man has created on this natural beauty, but by seeing all through loving, joyful eyes, you can't help but create the changes that are needed to heal this place you live in, and you will create actions that will create healing for your God-given beautiful surroundings.

Matthew 7

Love your neighbor as you would want them to love you. Don't criticize someone because they don't see things through the light of God's love. Help them by allowing them to see the light in your eyes and your actions. Your joy in life, your love in life can be infectious. If you choose to criticize them, darkness then surrounds you. Let your light be bright and those around will either feel the warmth, or not. It is of their choosing. Ask God to be a part of all your actions. Ask and you shall receive. You choose your own path. By letting God, and asking God, to be with you down this path, you can have all. You are creating every moment of your life moment-to-moment, so create what you want and ask God to guide you in your choices. All can have eternal life with God in his love. Simply choose to do so. Those that don't will live eternally in darkness.

There will be many who preach that they have all the answers to life and to follow them. They may even do so in the name of Jesus, but you must find God in your own heart. If one man says "this is the way" and another says "no, do this to fall into God's grace," then walk away. Simply ask God to be a part of all your conscious decisions, and answers will come. Simply ask and you shall receive. Don't fear to be inspired by those around you who teach the gospel. Be inspired, but never let one man's preachings be taken solely as God's word and follow blindly. Always open your eyes and ask God for guidance and you will receive it.

Matthew 8

In my life experience on earth, I performed what you say are healing miracles. Everyone is created by God and each has this capability within him. You are all created by God, so this means you all have this capability. To heal, you simply ask God to come into your presence and feel the warmth of his love and then pass this on, combined with the energy created by your own loving hands.

This takes a true commitment to your faith. Your own physicalness creates blockage for the loving, healing power to flow. You must clear your mind, feel God's presence, and visualize the healing process. It was easy for me to tap into this, for I knew exactly who I was and from where I came. I performed many healings, and those who were healed had great faith to let the power of God's love flow through them.

When I stopped the raging waters while at sea, I used this same process. I felt the strength of God's love, and then saw the winds calm and the sea smooth. Bring God into all experiences, ask to be surrounded by a divine white light, and feel the comfort it brings to any situation. Do this often and ask for a divine white light to surround your loved ones. Each and every day do this. Visualize each loved one as you ask God to surround them with this white light of protection. This is a wonderful way to experience those you love, every day, even if you are away from them. They can feel this moment of love if they are in tune with it; they can feel it consciously.

You create your own experiences. Knowing this, create all things with God's love around all things. Know it to be so, and the seas will calm and winds will cease, if this is what you truly want.

Matthew 9

It will be difficult for many to accept that this writing is coming from me, just as it was difficult for those who were preaching God's word during my time physically there. When I spoke that I was given the power by God to cast away your sins, they condemned me and said I was blaspheming against God. Religious leaders over time always use fear to lead you to God. It's a power that they try to hold over you. When it is made simple, all you have to do is have faith and trust in God. It's hard for many to accept, because there is no fear in the words that I speak. God doesn't want to have a hold on you because of your fear of what he will do or that he might strike you down. If this is what he wanted, would there be all the bad in the world? No, God would just strike down those who disobeyed him. Instead, God wants you to rejoice in his love and see the beauty that it can create in all things.

That is all I did. I cured many who were sick around me because of my faith, combined with their faith. This caused many to believe and follow me, but I did not do this to get them to follow me because of the magic I could perform. I simply showed that by living with God in your existence in this life, that all things are possible for each and every one of you.

Many fear this power that God gives to each individual, because they can't face the truth of the knowledge that God gave every man (and woman) free will to make their own choices. It is easier for those to say they believe from a distance, rather than to live day-to-day in the power of God's love. What I performed can be performed by anyone created by God (and all are created by God). "The harvest is so great; the workers are so few." Each and every one of you can have an impact on changing this; you can bring new workers to cultivate this harvest of God's great blessings. Each person who truly believes can have a major impact on those they come in contact with, and take joy in the good that is done.

Many criticized me for sharing much of my time with those whom others felt were unworthy of God's love. No one is unworthy and every living thing is important in this existence. Do God's work here on earth and pass this message on to others, even though many will let their fears say you are possessed by the devil. In reality no devil or darkness can stand up to the strength of God's loving hands. So pass this message on, and pray for all to find more meaning in their own lives through these words.

Matthew 10

I sent my twelve disciples out to teach God's love, and warned them that many would turn against them and persecute them; but if they would awaken just one child to the knowledge of living in God's love, they would be rewarded. This reward is not something as small as material wealth, but a worth that goes deep within their soul. I asked them not to worry about their physical well-being, but to keep their souls open to God's love; even if they lost their physical lives, they would have peace in the knowledge that they have everlasting and eternal life just by accepting and knowing God's presence and love. If you turn your back to his love, then you live in darkness of it.

Matthew 11

As I went and preached in the cities, John the Baptist could not believe that I was truly who I said I was. This is a man who preached of my coming, but had a difficult time knowing when he was face-to-face with me, just as you constantly question if this is me who is speaking to you now. And as I instructed John, just ask for God's guidance and believe in your faith. Truly believing is an easy thing said, but a hard thing to live day in and day out. Don't punish yourself for times of doubt; just move on, acknowledge it, and ask God for strength.

Your faith will see you through. With all the healing I performed (people called them miracles), people still doubted. They doubted even what they saw with their own eyes.

Shed your fears and walk where I have walked. Ask for my guidance and that of the Almighty Father, and step-by-step you shall find rest for your soul and peace in your life.

Matthew 12

Man makes many rules by what he thinks he knows is truth. Mankind should be less interested in rules and condemning those around them who break these rules, but instead fill their hearts and souls with God's love and act out of this. This love will be seen in their actions.

I spoke and talked to God each and every day. I did not need a special day to do this. He was and is a part of my every moment. When I healed on the Sabbath, the ministers of their day condemned me because they believed I was breaking God's law by working on the Sabbath. Every day can be the Sabbath. Don't stop loving and doing good deeds because someone tells you this is not the right day for this. Make each day a day in the life with God. Instead of seeing the good that was being done and praising and thanking God for the miracles I was performing through God, in fear they looked to rules they made. These became more important than God's love and the good that he can create every day.

This is why I came in the first place, to show mankind how they were losing God's message in their own, man-made ways of worship. When people fear, they react by trying to control. When action is created by fear, then you move further from God's message. Fear creates anger and controlling needs. When you react out of love, then there is no need to control another or to be more powerful than another. Action from fear is a human characteristic that has developed over time, and many react out of this need not even being fully conscious of why their actions are such. This is why I say, live consciously each and every moment in the light of God's love; then these fear-driven characteristics we develop won't have such a hold over us nor will we need to control, and the fears will subside.

When those I touched cast away their fears and were enlightened to God's loving arms, there were those who said I made people who were possessed by Satan cast away their demons, because I, myself, was Satan. This is just another example of their fears controlling their lives. You will see this in your own life, and there'll be those who will condemn these words and let their fears control their actions, just as then. But if one person finds the light of God's love in these words, and his actions come out of this conscious knowledge, it is contagious. And others will also see the light of this love, and so on. God has given you all complete free will to experience all. I say to you, it is far greater and more fulfilling to experience your life with the knowledge of God's love, and to have your actions and thoughts be created out of this conscious knowledge. Let your light shine brightly and you will truly be experiencing "heaven on earth."

Mankind keeps wanting more proof of God's presence. They want to see more miracles performed by me. I say to you, I could perform the most amazing miracles today and there will be those who say, "Now I believe." But when tomorrow comes and this miracle is just a memory, they again will question what they saw, and doubt. Miracles can be a part of your lives every day just by your trust and belief in God's graciousness, and by living fully in this knowledge and creating your life experiences through this knowledge.

All of mankind was created by God, so all are your brothers, sisters, mothers, and fathers under the greater kingdom of God. Know this and create your actions toward others out of this knowledge.

Matthew 13

In my teachings, I used many illustrations of living with the knowledge of God's love, and creating actions from the knowledge of this love. Those who listen and learn find these illustrations very meaningful in their lives. But there are many who hear the words, but don't understand. They will condemn the words and reject this knowledge of God's love. Those who hear it and create their actions from this knowledge grow strong, as does a seed in good soil with deep roots in this love. There will be those who say, yes, I believe; but when what they perceive as hardship falls upon them, they will run from these truths, just as a seed that grows on shallow soil is easily uprooted. When your time has come to leave this physical experience, with your deep-rooted knowledge of God's love, you will walk into the light and live forever in his loving presence. Those who turn against the light of this knowledge will live in darkness. Grow your roots deep into the knowledge of this love and create your actions from this love; you will have "heaven on earth," and always live in the knowledge of God's warmth and love eternally.

When I went back to my hometown of Nazareth, people marveled at my knowledge and miracles. But then they said, how can this be so, for my father was just a carpenter and they knew my family members. They then doubted what their own eyes had seen and what their own ears had heard. When the message is too simple or too easy to relate to, then it becomes hard for many to accept. It is easier to worship something they don't fully understand. It is easier to accept God's word, which was not written in their lifetime, so they can keep their faith at a distance rather than up close and personal. I ask you this: Has God stopped creating? Did God decide he could only perform miracles in the beginning of time? Christians every day say they believe in Jesus as the Son of God. They say they believe in angels, for they were taught that angels existed. They say they believe that Moses talked to a burning bush, which was God talking to Moses. But tell them God is talking to them today, just as before, just as Joseph had been told that he and Mary would parent the Lord Jesus, then they say okay, yes, I believe. But truly, if I speak, they deny that it is me. For it is easier to believe something that doesn't have to confront them right now, in the present.

Matthew 14

John the Baptist was beheaded and left this physical existence due to a promise by King

Herod. John was so committed to his belief and faith, that even in what appears to be great hardship, he understood and knew where he was going, even in losing his physical existence here. It is, many times, far greater pain for those who remain here to endure this loss of a friend or family member.

Even though I knew and understood John's faith had led him and kept him in God's great warmth and love, I was troubled at the news of his death and I experienced great grief in this knowledge. For God had given me the opportunity to experience all pain, happiness, fear, and anger just as with every one of you. But my constant communication with God, and the knowledge of his love, brought me through all experiences. When I heard the news, I went into the wilderness to be alone in my experience. Many followed and later I ran into more and continued my preaching and healing. With strong faith you can endure all pain, and with strong faith anything is possible. If you believe you can move mountains, you can move mountains.

When my disciples left to go back home across the waters, a storm came in and they were afraid as the seas grew stronger. I walked across the water to them in the early morning hours. When they recognized it was me, their fears subsided, for they were reminded that through God's love all is possible. I asked Peter to come out of the boat and take my hand. Peter also walked on the water, but as he looked around and saw the waves, he became frightened and started to sink. It is so easy in this world to get overwhelmed with the difficulties that face us each and every day; but with the knowledge of God's love and the total belief and commitment to this knowledge, all is possible.

So always ask and you shall receive. It is easy to have faith when you are sturdy on top of the water, but when your faith is tested and you are sinking, this is the time to call upon your faith and trust with great conviction, rather than to sink further and turn your back on God's powerful and everlasting love. I could calm the waters and stop the winds because I knew, without a doubt, that I was creating every moment from the knowledge of God's love, and kept asking him to be a part of every thought and action I created. You truly can choose your destiny from: first your thought, then your action, rooted from this knowledge. God has created all things and has given you free will to experience all. Your choices create your realities.

Matthew 15

The ministers of the Jewish faith at that time criticized me, for they said I disobeyed what they interpreted as God's laws; just as today you will be criticized for what you write. There will be many who will find you crazy, for it is far easier to denounce these words, than face them and live them. Just as the ministers lived their rituals, it was difficult for them to move away from their habits, even if they were proven that these rituals were man-made and not a commandment of God's. For there are no commandments from God, there are only commitments. If he was to command you and control your every move, then how can you then experience life? He instead made "commitments" to you, and if you let these "commitments" be a part of your life each and every day, then you will truly know you are living "heaven on earth."

Many times in my life I showed how you can feed many with just a little. Have faith and ask God to be a part of your living experience and you will never go hungry; you will always have plenty. If you believe this, you can create anything. All is possible.

Matthew 16

The leaders of the church during this time came to me and asked me to perform more miracles. I could perform miracle after miracle, but it would never be enough. They had to learn and perform miracles within their own lives. God gives us a chance to create our lives and choices every moment, but our fears and doubts keep us from experiencing these truths.

When I warned my disciples that many of the church leaders would not listen to these words and would criticize, then I made a mention of yeast and they mistook this to mean, because they had forgotten bread, to worry. Even my own disciples, who were around me all the time and faithfully followed me, many times could not fully grasp the power of God's creation and the bringing of his love and presence into all experiences consciously. What greatness could they achieve I asked them; did we not just feed thousands with just four loaves of bread? Worry and fear can stop us from truly becoming who we are and want to be. We say: If only I had this, I could do thus. When in reality, if you do thus you will have this. So I say to you, the experience you want to experience takes motion by doing.

I told my disciples that I would be killed in Jerusalem, but would rise again after three days and live eternally with my Father in heaven. Peter was angry and said I must stop this from happening, to use my powers and show them I was the Son of God. Peter was so wrapped up in the here and now of this existence, that he couldn't see that dying and rising again was more powerful in showing that there was far more to life than this physical experience we have here on earth. If you get so caught up in the ups and downs of this physical life experience, how do you fully become who your soul yearns to be? Know without any doubt that eternal life, in the knowledge of God's great love, is far greater than any monetary gains you have in this life experience. Enjoy your life experiences and bring God's love into all things. Create your actions and decisions from this knowledge, and you will experience "heaven on earth"; and any catastrophe you face, even physical death, won't be too great to bear, for those who live their lives with this knowledge of God's presence in all things will have everlasting life. With this knowledge enjoy all life's experiences, for you know you will be in the light of God's love eternally.

God has given you free will, but there are consequences that you may endure. Know that God has created all, and he never turns his back on you. If you turn your back on him, you might face difficult consequences; but know God has his hands open to you at all times. Turn to him and feel this warmth, and you can endure even the deepest pain. Without pain, how do you know what joy is? God has created all, and you are to choose. By knowing of God's love and accepting his love, your actions will be created out of this knowledge. Let God be a part of your decisions, and you will experience a deep love in all things. God does not punish you; follow his teachings and avoid much of the pain that is created by the consequences of actions that are not created out of this love.

Matthew 17

I took Peter, James, and John to a wonderful mountaintop. You could feel God's beauty all around you. I asked for God to circle me with a divine white light (as I did daily), always asking to keep the negative and the darkness away, and the bright light of God's love around me. Peter, James, and John saw this light, and as I was speaking to God, Moses and Elijah appeared, for I often had conversations with those who were on a different plane than the physical existence at that moment. Peter, James, and John were excited to see these great prophets. Then God spoke to me and the three of them heard loud and clear. They fell to their knees and were afraid. I went to them, touched them, and said don't be afraid. When they looked at me, I was alone. But again, they had seen with their own eyes souls that had previously lived physical lives here on earth, and they had heard God speak.

God speaks to us every day, just not in quite the dramatic fashion they experienced that day. But they were able to see that souls live on, not just in this physical presence. They believed this to be true before, but when it was actually presented to them so clearly, they still fell to their knees in fear when God spoke. Souls can live more than one life in physical form, here on what you call earth. For John the Baptist, they came to realize, had in fact lived before as Elijah. Early Scriptures spoke that Elijah would come before I came into this physical life. Elijah came, but no one recognized him, and in fact they persecuted him and killed him, just as they did to me.

Dave, you have also lived here before and know this to be true, even though you struggle with this and have a hard time with this. Don't fear this news, rejoice in it; know that life is a constant awakening to new challenges to experience. You, in fact, came back into this existence for the purpose of writing this message, although you have only, in recent years, let yourself open up to this knowledge; and today you still doubt and question. But that is okay. Each and every day that you write, the message comes through more strongly and clearly.

When Peter, James, John, and I returned from the mountaintop, a man came and asked for me to cure his son. He had first asked the disciples to heal his son, but the son was not healed. I healed him in that instant, as they could have healed him if it were not for self-doubt (just as now, when you are writing, you question, "Are you really speaking with me, and are my words the ones that are appearing on this page?"). You can move mountains, if only you believe. It was at this time I told my disciples that my time in this existence was growing short. I would be betrayed and killed, but would arise again after three days.

Yes, I know you have a hard time with the fact that you once lived on earth before. You were tossing and turning in your sleep, because you are having a hard time dealing with the fact that this has been brought up in the book. You fear that people will think you are crazy for believing this. Stop worrying so much about what others will think of you. Let your faith guide you and ask God to be a part of your thoughts and a part of this writing. Those who want to feel God's great love through these words, will, and those who don't, won't.

When you walked on this earth before, you had the same worries. You couldn't tap into your healing powers because doubt and fear blocked you. But look at what you have accomplished in this lifetime. Was not what happened between you and your son Daniel proof enough? You constantly are healing your family. Your wife, Cathy, is very receptive to this healing power. Can't you see and feel the effect it has had on her? You still deny what took place after your car accident. Do you not remember when you were at the hospital? The doctor told you that you had a broken hip and your legs were broken in many places. Then during the transfer from one hospital to another, you felt the power of God's healing love like you had never felt before. You felt the bright light of God and even saw it; but you chose to forget it, until these words were written right now. You question, how could it be so, that once you arrived at the next hospital, you no longer had any broken bones? Were the first doctors just wrong? No, but you keep this exceptional miracle of God's healing power to yourself. Now you have shared it with your wife because she believes so thoroughly; but you are afraid to tell others because you are afraid they won't believe you and will think that you are crazy.

Share this story with love in your heart, and those who want to feel the warmth it brings, will, and those who don't, won't. When you lived before, you were the same soul then that you are now. You experienced the same fears that you do now. When I told my disciples I was going to be betrayed and killed, they were so afraid. They all worried about how they could go on with the great messages I brought, without me constantly by their side reminding them that what they were experiencing was real. Well, remember: I am constantly by your side, and in times of doubt and worry, ask me to comfort you, and ask for God's great arms to wrap around you and comfort you.

Matthew 18

The disciples wanted to know who among them would be greatest in God's eyes. I told them, those who can humble themselves as a little child. Have you ever seen the way a baby looks at you with such admiration and love? Cast away trying to be this or that, and trying to be better than another man. Those who can look into God's eyes with the all-loving eyes of a child will be the greatest in heaven. Help the children keep this unconditional love, by giving them unconditional love.

You are having problems with this chapter of the Bible, because the interpretations have warped the words. One moment it says God wants you to forgive seventy-times-seven, and the next it tells you God will send you to the torture chambers if you don't forgive, when I have already said God will never turn his back on you. It is you who decides to turn your back on God. God is all-forgiving. God gave you life in this physical life form to experience life. If you choose to experience something that is with your back to God's love, then you will also experience the consequences of that. God's words get turned a little here and a little there, so those who live their lives in fear can control another. Simply live your life in God's love and choose your actions from this knowledge. This does not mean that if you choose not to act out of love, that God will damn you for all eternity. He simply shows you how wonderful choices and actions are when created from this love within your soul, and simply shows the great power it has over all things. To truly know what "up" is, you have to know, first, what "down" is. God created all. Make conscious choices with this knowledge and you can experience "heaven on earth."

You can teach your children to obey you, because they fear what you will do to them. But, is it not a far greater experience for these children to obey you because it brings them great joy and because of the love they have for you? This is how God wants us to enjoy the great gift of life we all have, for he rejoices in your rejoices. When you feel great and wonderful, it is a wonderful experience, one that he enjoys experiencing also. When you feel frustrated and angered at the destruction mankind has brought upon this earth, God feels frustrated and angered, for he has created all and feels all. But God does not hate; and we are all here to help, and to show you the way to find out who you really are, and to enjoy the feeling it brings when you are in touch with this. Damages that have been done, when actions are created away from this, can be overcome.

When more than two or three are gathered in this knowledge and knowingly send out this loving energy, you can create changes.

Matthew 19

Marriage is a wonderful way to unite two souls and to father and mother children. It is not for all, and God does not condemn those who don't experience marriage. Marriage should be an everlasting commitment of two souls. The sharing of this special experience is wonderful, and a wonderful way to bring children into this world. You should constantly grow together, sharing your growth and the knowledge that you learn with each other. During difficult times, ask God's love to surround you and bring you through the rocky experiences. When two live together as husband and wife, know that there will be differences that will occur that create momentary difficulties in your relationship. But know that if you bring God's love into your marriage, both in the good times and the bad experiences, you can grow and blossom together and create a wonderful atmosphere for your children, and God's children, to grow and learn about life and God's love. If a husband and wife decide to divorce, it can bring great hardship on both the man and woman, and can create difficult experiences for the children. But again I say, God does not turn his back on you if this is what you choose to experience. And, if you decide to marry again, bring God's love into that marriage, and create your relationship and actions from this, through good times and bad times.

Many times I have been asked, how do you

get to heaven? Simply acknowledge heaven and the light of God's love. I keep saying, you can have "heaven on earth." I truly mean it. It is not how much you have in material things that creates a great joy deep within your soul, but experiencing all through God's love and creating your actions from this can. This does not mean it is wrong to have material riches, but know that true blissfulness and happiness comes from how you create your actions and when these actions are created from whom you truly want to be. I said that if you truly want to feel the power of God's love in all experiences, you should be willing to give up earthly possessions. If it becomes important for you to know who you truly want to be, don't let riches stand in your way. Simply enjoy material wealth for what it is, but never put material wealth above living in God's love if you truly want to live "heaven on earth."

What I mean by "heaven on earth" is knowing who you are and living with conscious choices in your experiences. This will bring you to experiences that are the most powerful and wonderful that you can possibly know. God created you in this physical form to experience all. When you truly know this, every experience in this life is more meaningful; and when you feel the magnificence of this, God feels and experiences the magnificence of this also.

My disciples asked me what reward they would receive for following me and leaving their families to do so. Their only reward was the experience it brought them. And, if this truly brought them closer to whom their soul longed to be, and brought them closer to the knowledge of God's love, and by living experiences with this knowledge, then there could be no greater reward. For living in the knowledge of God's loving light is truly living "heaven on earth."

Matthew 20

Another illustration that I used was that of an owner of an estate who hired help, and he told them he would pay them a penny for the day. They were happy to get the work and took the job gladly. When the owner later in the day hired more help and paid them the full penny, even though they worked fewer hours, the ones who were hired earlier became angry. This is an example of how we let ourselves get away from living our experiences created from love and not fear. In this case, fear that someone else was getting more for less effort. The workers who were hired earlier were happy to have the job and worked with this feeling until they let anger enter in because the land owner was generous to those he hired later. A good experience and a good feeling became a bad experience and a bad feeling. The message here is to rejoice in your life and the feelings of creating your actions from a love base. When anger slips in, for whatever reason, simply stop, acknowledge the anger, ask God to surround you, and feel the presence of his love. Don't get bogged down in what others might have that you don't. Rejoice in what you have and live life to its fullest, and thank God for each and every experience. Ask him daily to be a part of all your experiences and creations. He is always, but now be conscious of it. Ask him to help you create your actions with this knowledge.

At this time in my life, I told the disciples

what was going to take place shortly; that I would be betrayed by the chief priest and other Jewish leaders, and would be turned over to the Roman government. I would be crucified, but would rise again in three days. They all wanted to know if they could sit at my side in heaven and be leaders in heaven. To lead you must serve. I did not come to lead, but came to serve. When you truly understand this, then you can teach many.

Matthew 21

When I was coming into Jerusalem, I asked Peter and John to go ahead and bring me the colt of a donkey, for I wanted people to see that you didn't have to be carried in a fancy chariot and covered in gold to be a teacher and leader of people. Humble yourself and enjoy the giving you put out, and rejoice in the feeling that this experience gives you. To be a great leader in the eyes of God, humble yourself and truly enjoy the experience of giving and receiving.

As I came into the city, great crowds gathered and rejoiced in the occasion. As I went into the temple, tax collectors and merchants were exchanging money and selling their wares. I became angry (remember, I, as are you, was given the freedom to experience all), and I drove them out of the sanctuary. For a sanctuary is the place to meditate and have quiet time, to fully understand who you are and your relationship with God. Everyone needs quiet time just to be with God and themselves, to let the busy hustle and bustle of this life experience pass them by for awhile. This helps to ground you, and to remember who you are and want to be. Take the time; the experience can be quite blissful. After the merchants cleared out, I healed many, and many were rejoicing in the knowledge of God's presence in all things. The church leaders saw these miracles, and saw the joy it was bringing to so many. Instead of rejoicing in this as well, they became fearful. Again, as I have said before, it is much easier to believe in something that is not up close and happening right before your very own eyes. Even though this went right along with their very teachings, they couldn't handle this when it was happening right in front of their own eyes, and chose to reject me rather than rejoice with me in the power of God's great love.

I told them that evil men and prostitutes would have an easier time truly accepting God's love and stepping into the light when it was presented to them. All anyone has to do is accept this knowledge, and when God reaches his hand to you, simply accept and rejoice in this love. The priests spent so much time in telling what God would do, if you did this or that, that they couldn't recognize him when he was standing right in front of them. Just simply open up your hearts and create your experience from this loving place, and you will rejoice in the feeling it brings.

Matthew 22

In my final days living on earth, I told many stories to illustrate God's kingdom. All the Pharisees were interested in was finding a way to rid themselves of me. But to all who listened, it was rejoicing news to them, and they created their life experiences with this knowledge. God has opened his doors for all to experience life, and he experiences life through each and every soul. You are all a part of his family. Simply accept this and take heart in this knowledge, and let your actions stem from this knowledge.

I was asked if the people should pay taxes to the Roman empire. I said, show me a coin; they did, and I asked whose picture was on it. They said Caesar, and I said, then give the coin to Caesar and give all else to God. The Pharisees were more interested in trying to trick me into saying something that they could condemn me for, rather than truly listening and understanding the meaning of my replies.

The Sadducees, who did not believe in resurrection after death, asked me if there was life after death, and one of them, who had married several times, asked who in heaven would be their spouse. I simply told them that they were ignorant of what eternal life in God's love and grace was. Marriage is an experience of this physical life, but in heaven (or life not in this physical form), there is no marriage as we experience here. As to the question, is there resurrection of the dead? There is no God, if there is no resurrection. For God is not the God of the dead, but God of the living.

I was then asked which of the commandments (which I call "commitments") are most important? Love yourself, God, and all things with all your heart and soul. This was the first commitment and most powerful. Also, love your neighbor as much as yourself. When you truly experience this, then all of God's commitments stem from this, and your actions, which are generated by this knowledge, will fulfill all of his commitments.

I asked the Pharisees, "Who is the son of God?" They replied, "The Messiah, Son of

David." I asked them then, in the Scriptures they've read, does David not say God calls his Son Lord? If they believe in the Scriptures, then is not his Son a part of God, living life physically and experiencing life physically, just as he does in each and every one of you?

For you all agree, God created each and every one of you. You, then, are a part of God; each with individual souls and individual free will choices on how you want to live your life and create your life experiences. When you live your life and choose your actions from the commitments that were handed down to Moses, then you truly can experience "heaven on earth." By knowing who you are, and knowing who Jesus and God are, and by opening your eyes to this, you create your life choices totally differently than if you don't. For knowing this, you know you have eternal life, and this physical existence at this time is only a segment of your eternal existence. By simply knowing this, you create actions from love (God's love—your love) rather than from fear and anger.

They asked me no further questions after that.

Matthew 23

The church leaders of that day tried to be like Moses, presenting law after law to obey. They loved the power it gave them over other human beings. Some of their laws were not bad to follow, but others were man-made and used to control. Notice that I said "their" laws. Church leaders still today love to create laws, and then point to scripture, pulled out of context, to show that "their" way is the best. They feed on the power it gives them over others. Just as in the days that I walked on earth, the majority of them could never keep to these laws in their own personal lives. But yes, they were quick to condemn others.

God's plan is simple—for you to experience life in the physical form. Humble yourself. Don't try to be better than another man; be better within yourself. Those whom you come in contact with will feel God's love within your presence if you truly create your actions from this place. If you experience something that takes you away from this place, simply ask God to guide you, and let him be a part of all your conscious thinking. God will never turn his back on you; it is you who turns away from God. God does not want you to act out of fear for what he might do to you, but instead wants you to make choices and create actions out of his great love of life and love for you. Many church leaders would want you to believe differently, so "they," not God, have a hold over you, boosting them up high and mighty. It is far greater to serve humbly, with great joy in your heart, than to be high and mighty with a sorrowful heart.

The outside of a cup can be shiny and beautiful, but if the inside is dirty, then drinking from this cup is not pleasant. Too many church leaders of this time and that, look good and shine on the outside, but inside, they are filthy. It is far greater to experience life from the inside, than worry so much about what the outside looks like to others. Truly live with conscious thought of God's love and create your actions from this place, and the outside will take care of itself.

Church leaders today will look at these words and say they cannot be from Jesus, their Lord, for this reason or that. They won't even be aware that they are acting and living just like the Pharisees and the church leaders who crucified me, as their fathers before them crucified other prophets. For some reason, from the beginning of man and woman walking on this earth, it has always been easier to follow and believe in something that happened in the past, rather than to believe in what they can see and touch right in front of them. For they let fear guide them, rather than love—deep-rooted love. For God has never stopped creating and performing miracles. Why would the Creator, God the Father/Mother, God who is all there is, simply stop creating and stop communicating? Instead, mankind finds it simply too frightening to believe that what occurred during the time I was on earth, or Moses before me, could take place today as well.

Is it not amazing that a man or woman can say they study the Scriptures and live by the Scriptures (read Matthew 23) and be blind to the message that still comes through today, even through thousands of years and many interpretations. They are creating their actions from the same place that they condemned the church leaders of that day. For I say these same people who say they love me would crucify me today just as the Pharisees did. It is so easy to point a finger, but hard to look within.

When you have doubt and don't know what to believe, simply ask for God to be with you and to be a part of your decisions and actions. See how it feels to you, not what someone else tells you that it should feel like. Do this each and every day. Know that your salvation is guaranteed and that God's love is "unconditional." Then, if you stumble with an action created from a place that you didn't want to be a part of, simply get up and create a new action without fear, for you have everlasting life simply by knowing that you do. I said I am the way, simply know me, and you shall have everlasting life. You will have everlasting life either in the light of God's love or in darkness.

Matthew 24

The end of this world can come at anytime. Know that God is love. When I appear again, it will be to reach out. Those who know God and know me will be lifted into all the glories of heaven. This is not something to fear; live your life and enjoy your life experiences, create healing in your world. There has been so much hate and destruction that this world can't take much more; but if you and your brother next to you and your son and those around you, each start creating a healing love and sending it out, this world can go on and on. Remember you have the power to move mountains. Open your eyes to the healing powers of God's love. Whenever there are those gathered in my name, the power generated and created is magnificent. So read these words and don't cower down in fear, but stand tall and start this moment creating healing to this world; and be a light that starts a flame that beams the brightness of God's love more magnificently than any fire has ever burned before.

When Matthew wrote these words, yes, he was inspired by me. But he also was very, very angry at the crucifixion and the way leaders of the church denounced me and were so very hypocritical. That is why hate sometimes takes over these words. God is love, and again I say, he will never turn his back on you. It is your choice to receive this love and be inspired by it, or to turn away from it.

Matthew 25

Everlasting life is assured to all. But know this: To live everlasting in the light and knowledge of God's love, you must know God's love. To know God's love is to live in conscious knowledge of God's love, and to create your actions from this knowledge. Those who don't are in darkness, and in darkness they will remain.

Matthew 26

It came time for the Passover, and I told my disciples that after two days I would be betrayed and crucified. The chief priests were assembled at that moment, deciding how to capture me, kill me, and keep the masses from having an uproar. This was the time when I had the last supper, broke the bread, and said, "Eat, this is my body, and take the wine and drink, this is my blood; do this in remembrance of me." I told them that one of them had betrayed me. Judas asked if it was him, and I replied, "Yes." He had negotiated with the chief priests to hand me over for thirty pieces of silver.

I told the disciples that they would desert me and scatter. Peter said that there was no way he would leave my side. He told me he would rather die by my side. I told him he would deny that he even knew me, three times before the sunrise the following day. I took John, James,

and Peter to a garden grove, called Geth-
semane. While the disciples waited outside the
garden, I laid, face down, praying to God to
give me the courage to endure the pain and
great sorrow I was about to face; for I was in
human form and experienced the same feelings
that every man does who walks this earth. I was
afraid, and asked God to keep me strong.

When they came to take me, the soldiers
were armed, and it was a terrifying experience.
The disciples scattered, as I had said they
would. A sword was drawn, and cut off the ear
of one of the high priest's servants. I said, "Put
away the sword." Could I not have God stop
this, this very instant?

I knew I had to die and arise again, to show
that there is no end at the time of death, but
only eternity with God, the Father. When the
angry mob took me away, they took me to the
high priest and asked if I claimed to be the Son
of God, the Messiah. I said, "Yes," and they
sentenced me to death. It was a very angry
scene, with everyone yelling. There was so
much hate all around.

Then a girl came to Peter and said, "I know
you. You are one who was with Jesus." Peter
answered, no, that he didn't even know me.
Two other times, Peter was recognized as one
of my followers, but both times, again, he
denied he knew me. The fear overwhelmed
him, and when the sun arose, he realized he
had done exactly as I had told him he would.
Matthew watched in hiding, also consumed by
fear.

In this physical form, fear is very powerful
over the human body. That is why you must
constantly ask for God's strength when fear

empowers you. Even those with the greatest of intentions can be bound by fear. Circle yourself with a divine white light, and ask God to fill the light with the warmth of his love, and to keep the darkness and negativity away; ask for his love to give you strength to endure all.

I feel great sorrow as I write these last few chapters of Matthew. It is clearly affecting my mood. At times during this writing, I have felt elated and so very inspired. I guess that is what is meant by "to experience joy, you must know what sorrow feels like."

Matthew 27

When morning came, they took me to Pilate, the governor. They took me in chains, asking if I should be put to death. When Judas saw me in chains and heard they had condemned me to death, he couldn't bear what he had done. He didn't want the money, and couldn't even look at it. He thought the money could bring him great joy, but now knew, without any doubt, that what he had done was wrong, and not a part of what he wanted to be. The consequences of his actions caused him such grief that he returned the money to the priest. They wouldn't accept it, because it was money spent on murder, and it was against their law to accept it. Judas was so disgusted with himself, he threw the money at them and turned away from God, for he couldn't even look at himself, let alone God; and he killed himself and lives in darkness.

Even with such a terrible deed that he had

done, if he had turned to God to endure the great pain he felt, God would have been there for him with open arms. If you think this means that you can do whatever you want and God will always be there for you, well, this is true. But you must understand the consequences. It might sound easy for you to just rush into God's open arms, but the reality of the situation is, when you act with your back to God, it is not as easy as you think to turn back suddenly and find the light of God's love. By living in and surrounding your daily actions in God's love, it is so very easy to walk into the light of his love because you experience it daily and know how it feels. When you act away from this, it is difficult to experience, because you don't know what it is like when it is right in front of you. Judas let monetary physical desires start dictating his actions, and slipped away from God without even being aware of it. He had a rude awakening when he saw me in chains and the priest crucifying me. I would love for Judas' soul to turn back to the light. The priest ended up taking the thirty pieces of silver, buying land where clay was used for pots, and made it into a cemetery for foreigners who died in Jerusalem, which is known as the "field of blood."

When I stood before Pilate, I was asked if I was the Messiah. I replied, "Yes." As the Jewish leaders made their many accusations against me, I remained silent. Pilate asked me, "Don't you hear what they are saying?" He felt I should defend myself against these accusations. The custom for Pilate during the Passover was to release one Jewish prisoner. During this particular time, there was a very notorious criminal, known as Barabbas. He asked the crowd, who he should release, and the crowd, brought to almost riot conditions by the Jewish leaders, said to release Barabbas and crucify this false god, Jesus. Pilate simply took a bowl of water and washed his hands and said, "I wash my hands, for the blood of this decent man will be on you," and they yelled in a frenzy: "Crucify, crucify!"

The soldiers took me away and stripped me of my clothing and put a thorn crown upon my head and mocked me, saying, "Hail to the King of the Jews." It was physically painful, but I felt more sorrow for the anger and the hate that the men around me were engulfed in. I kept asking for strength from God, and prayed for enlightenment for those around me who were with so much hate and anger.

As the soldiers lead me out, I tripped and fell, so they grabbed a man from the crowd and had him carry my cross. When we reached the hill, they nailed me to the cross, between two other prisoners whom they were crucifying that day. The soldiers continued to mock me and put a sign over my head saying, "King of the Jews." Many angry people spat on me and said, "If you are the Son of God, then come down from the cross; show us your powers." The high priests were so proud of themselves. They said, "He could save others, but can't save himself." They went to Pilate and warned him that I had said I would arise from the dead after three days. They asked Pilate to seal my tomb and put guards out in front, so my disciples wouldn't steal my body and claim that I had arisen.

As I was on the cross, I felt every bit of pain and sorrow, as any human would. Even though

I knew deep within my soul I had to leave this human form to show God's wonderful love of eternal life, it was difficult to endure. Just before I passed on, when I thought I could not take it any longer, I yelled to God, "Why have you forsaken me?" and then shortly thereafter, I passed on. At that moment, the curtain in the temple was split and the earth shook. The soldiers who had been mocking me felt great fear and said surely he must be the Son of God. The day had gotten dark and the earth shook. Those who had died before appeared to many in the city. Joseph of Arimathea went to Pilate and asked to cleanse my body and prepare it for burial—to wrap it in white cloth. Pilate allowed him to, and afterward, they sealed the tomb and sent soldiers out front to protect it from intrusion.

Matthew 28

On Sunday morning, three days later, my mother Mary and the other women went to the tomb. When they got there, there was a great earthquake and the stone was rolled aside, and an angel of the Lord sat upon it. The soldiers were so frightened that they fainted in fear. The angel spoke to the two Marys and told them I had arisen, and to tell the disciples to go to Galilee and that Jesus would speak to them there. As they were leaving, very frightened but also filled with joy, they ran right into me. We hugged, and I told them to get the others and meet in Galilee. I told them to let their fears abate, to ask God to comfort them and give them strength.

When the guards told the Jewish priest what had happened, they were too proud to believe it. They were so caught up in their righteousness, that they couldn't bear to believe. They told the soldiers not to repeat the story, and that the disciples had taken the body when they were asleep. Think about this. The stone was sealed and guarded. Yet the priests needed so desperately to believe in themselves that they actually somehow believed this to be the case, even if it was physically impossible. This is what is still happening today. God's wonderful appearances and love are everywhere, but those who refuse to see it or feel it, still reject it.

When I met the disciples, it was hard for them to believe it was truly me. But I told them to believe in the Father, Son, and Holy Ghost; that I am the living example that the messages I taught are true. I told them to go out and spread the message; baptize others into the knowledge they have learned through me. I will be with you always, each and every step of the way, and know there is a place for you when you leave this physical plane. Teach others the commitments that God has given to all mankind. Have them create their actions out of love, and always ask God to be a part of all things. He always is, but knowing it creates the actions that brings you to who your spirit longs to be.

chapter 7

Revelation

During this entire process of writing with Jesus, and since I had begun with Genesis, I felt a desire from deep within driving me to write on Revelation, the last book of the Bible. I had always found the Book of Revelation to be contradictory to the image I held of God. I spoke with various ministers to get their opinions and read everything I could get my hands on to shed some light on this book of the Bible. It's interesting to note here that many churches spent the entire final year of this past century studying Revelation. What I found was that Revelation seems to be the area in the Bible where people have the greatest differences of opinion.

In a conversation with a minister whom I hold in very high regard, I came to believe that the John who authored Revelation was not the disciple John who wrote the books of John in the New Testament. In fact, it appears that Revelation was written long after the disciple John had passed away, and that the John who wrote Revelation did so while imprisoned by the Romans. He was extremely angry and bitter and was letting the Romans know that they would suffer, and that God would strike them down when all evil was finally conquered. It was he who would receive all the gold and riches, because he had been faithful to God and had suffered for God. As I have mentioned, this is a perfect example of biblical interpretation where we need to look at what was going on in the author's own personal life when he wrote the words, and where we need to be aware of what influences he personally brought into those writings.

When I told a friend of mine the problems I had with accepting Revelation as my truth, his response was, "Then what is the point of being a Christian and bearing all this suffering?" He went on to say, "Revelation was the Rapture, it was the final 'touchdown!'" I read through Revelation again, and asked Jesus to help me understand what was written there. For those of you who share my friend's feelings, maybe after reading this book you may find another reason for being a Christian: one that doesn't mean you are required to suffer.

Jesus is here. Go ahead.

In my teachings, while I walked on earth, is this what I preached? At any time did I make these statements? Did I ever present our Father

God in this light? There are those who grab onto the Book of Revelation and try to please God because of what is written there. If this is the message that is from God, then why did I not preach it?

This book is as far from the truth of the message I bring as it can possibly be. If this is the message I was to bring, would I have not shown it to you all? I came *because* of these controlling types of messages that were being presented as God's Word. If you believe in me and the God the Father that I spoke of, then you can't possibly believe in the image of God and heaven presented in the Book of Revelation. If you find the Book of Revelation confusing and contradictory to the wonderful relationship you all can have with an all-loving God, then walk away from the words that were presented there. They are not from God; they are man-made and presented there because of anger—but not God's anger. Religions today, as before, are so wrapped up in doctrines and rules that they stray many times from my simple teachings. When you want answers, simply pray and communicate with God. The author of Revelation was very angry at being held prisoner and he stopped creating his thoughts and actions from a love base. He wanted those who held him captive to know that God would punish them severely.

I know you wonder how did this Book of Revelation become a part of the Bible? Just as many words of fear, and of the Lord's wrath, have been presented in other parts of the Bible, they were put in by those that were angered by my crucifixion, rather than rejoicing in the eternal life that we all are given. Some of my final words were, "God forgive them, for they know not what they have done and are in darkness of the true light of God's love." I did not say, "God strike these people down because of what they have done to me." I prayed for those souls to be brought into the light of God's love, and to cast away their fear which created the anger that caused them to crucify me.

Yet there are those who strive to do good deeds, and want to be rewarded for their good deeds and see that those who stray get severely punished. But this is not how I lived or what I taught. Always go back to my simple teachings and my life when you are faced with something as contradictory as the Book of Revelation is to a God who loves unconditionally—one who doesn't keep score on your good deeds. Do good deeds simply because it makes you joyous, and you love the joy it brings to others.

chapter 8

God's Promises

At this point, I felt I had covered enough material regarding specific books of the Bible. The writings went on from there to general areas that affect our everyday lives. Those with whom I shared the next few chapters would always find such great comfort and joy in what was written. They would begin to take off the gloves of debate, and just allow the words to inspire them.

Jesus is here. Go ahead.

There is no fear in loving and experiencing God in all things. This does not mean you won't, from time to time, be fearful of some physical condition taking place in your life. This statement is more geared to those who have been taught to "fear" God; to do good or he will strike you down. God simply created you to experience all; and to experience all, you have been created with complete free will. God has given you "commitments" whereby, if you live your life creating your experiences out of love, and live day-to-day the ten "commitments" he passed on through Moses, your life can be joyous and your soul can attain who it longs to be. When you get off this path, the consequences are that life is not as fulfilling while you are here in this physical form.

God will never turn his back on you. God loves unconditionally. I came to teach these truths. Create your actions from your love of life, love of God, and love of yourself. Raise your children in the same way. Don't teach them to do right in your eyes or you will strike them down. Show them and give them love. When they create their actions from a love base instead of fear, you will rejoice in their decisions and actions.

Have you not noticed that the greatest criminals on earth are ones who were raised in fear and anger? Why then do some churches, who say they are speaking my teachings, control their followers with fear of the Lord? There are those who say that "fear the Lord" in the Bible means "respect the Lord." Fear and respect are at different ends. Do you respect someone because you fear them? I say it again: God's love is unconditional. He will never turn his back on you. Open up to him and communicate with him daily and rejoice in this.

Know that you have eternal life. I came to earth and was crucified to show that there is so much more than this physical existence that you are now living. Rejoice in this knowledge, and create your actions knowing that you have everlasting life in the warmth of God's love just by knowing this. There is no checklist of good deeds you must perform. Do the good deeds for the experience and joy it can bring you. When you are tempted to do something that will gain you some satisfaction for that moment, but will take you further from God's truths, then walk away from that decision. If you, step-by-step, start living consciously each and every day knowing and creating your actions and realities from love, your life will take on more meaning than you ever dreamed possible.

Spend time, and make time, to experience natural beauties. Go to the mountains, beaches, and forests. Take in the beauty that God has created. Let it rejuvenate your soul. If you take time to enjoy these beautiful natural surroundings that God has created, it will take you further from the hustle and bustle of this life, and will help you to put back into perspective what is really important. Find peaceful areas and sit for awhile, and simply let God's love take you to highs you never dreamed possible.

Take a moment to close your eyes and remember the feeling you had the first time someone whom you truly cared about said, "I love you." Let yourself feel the warmth, the elation, and the exhilarating feeling it brings to you. Know that you are loved. Let that warmth, elation, and exhilaration sweep over your body. Know I will always be with you, through hard times and good times. Feel me deep within your soul. I will be there.

When things get tough and confusing, take time to stop and feel my presence, so I can comfort you. Bring me in, too, when you are completely elated, so we can rejoice together. I will always be there. You are never alone.

Don't wait to die to go to heaven; follow these teachings and start living "heaven on earth" now. Collective thought and collective prayer can mend this world. Keep gathering and sharing God's love. Changes can and will take place. Create new healing in this world. Don't wait until later for something you can create now; start at this very moment. Too often people say they are going to do something they have always wanted to do, once they have the time. Do it now, and you will have the time.

When you are faced with the hardship this life can bring, take heart that I am with you every step of the way. I want to be your closest friend. Know that I am always with you, and that I am open to a glorious one-on-one relationship with you. There are also guides and angels, and they look forward to helping you through tough times and good times as well; just simply ask. When you are completely overwhelmed, and you don't know how you are going to make it, just ask for help and you too can "walk on water." Don't run when it feels like you are sinking. Keep your faith strong, and before you know it, you will be standing tall on top again.

Take time for spiritual healing each and every day. Your life can be so much more fulfilling. In today's world with faxes, cell phones, and e-mail, all these gadgets that supposedly give you time to accomplish more, ask yourself, has it really given you more time, or does it seem you have even less time? I say, take five to ten minutes each day to spend alone quietly with me. You will be more productive and will create far more meaningful accomplishments in your life, in those five to ten minutes, than you can in the rest of your day.

Ask for help in all that you do, whether it is a business meeting you are about to go into, a problem you are dealing with at home, or even just a quiet moment by yourself. Take a few moments to bring God into all experiences. You will rejoice in the way you handle each new situation.

Take time to pass love on to others whom you come in contact with. Every day, spend a quiet loving moment with each of the family members you live with, even if it is just a 30 second hug, and telling them how much you appreciate their love, and how proud you are to have them as a wife, husband, son, daughter, father, or mother. Take the time to pass on love.

A simple prayer for each and every day.
Thank you Lord for this day.
Help me to see your loving presence in all things.
Help me to create my actions from love.
Circle me with a divine white light,
help me to let the negatives go
and keep the positives within.
Thank you God.

chapter 9

Daniel—A True Life Miracle

Before I realized that these writings with Jesus would ultimately be put into a book for all to read, my wife was pregnant with our fourth child. As had become the custom in our home, we would go directly to Jesus to ask about personal matters within our family life. The first writing in this chapter was done after we found out we were having yet another son. What follows after that is the story of a "true life miracle" that happened directly to us.

It was almost two months prior to the time that Daniel was to be born, when my wife noticed that he had not been moving or kicking in two days. I was out of town on business, but she asked me to write with Jesus on June 3 to see if we should be concerned. The next writing that I share with you was done on June 4, while I was on a plane rushing home to be at their side. I have also included two more writings, one on

June 5 and then again on June 8, which dealt directly with those first few days of his life.

After reflecting on these events of the recent past, I truly believe that they all occurred for a very special reason. The entire experience has given me great strength and courage in both my faith and my willingness to share these beliefs with others publicly. This experience has given me a rock-solid foundation from which to draw upon, and the courage to share with others the faith in our abilities to heal. Without a shadow of a doubt, I came to know that I had to share these writings from Jesus with others outside my family, even if it meant being misunderstood and losing credibility or respect, from those who would have a hard time accepting my claim that these words indeed come directly from Jesus. I take a lot of strength from 1 Corinthians 5:3, where it is written: "Even though I am not physically present, I am always with you in spirit." Let this spirit in your life speak loud and clear, then be willing to be quiet and listen.

Jesus is here. Go ahead.

Yes, it's a boy. Daniel is a good name. May your children help this world with love and kindness.

Love your children fully, as they are seeds to transforming the world. They will need every bit of their strength and leadership ability to right "the damage" that has been done. It is not accurate to say "the wrong," because God created all, so that all can be experienced. However, people need to become more aware of "the damage" they have done from their own darkness or lack of knowledge. The consequences of this are that some of the wonderful creations of God can be destroyed, and it will take these seeds that he has planted and entrusted to you to help create healing in the world.

June 3

Jesus is here. Go ahead.

Daniel is fine. He is getting ready to enter this world, and would like to do so now. He is ready and is growing fine.

June 4

Jesus is here. Go ahead.

Daniel will be born tonight and will amaze everyone. He will grow strong and wise. Cathy will come through this just fine. Keep sending healing and love.

Love your wife with all your heart. She is fine and your baby will make it. Keep the faith. He will bring great joy. See the strength in him as he miraculously grows strong and wise.

June 5

Jesus is here and is always here.

Direct your healing with love to his brain and muscular strength. He will come through.

June 8

Jesus is here. Go ahead.

Daniel, the "Champion," is getting stronger all the time. The doctor will be pleased with the results. There will be some minor concerns, but nothing Daniel won't overcome. He will bring you great strength. June 4 is important because that is when Daniel decided he wanted to enter your lives. He did not want to wait any longer, the timing was right. Your lives will be filled with great joy from this child, as with all your children; each is special in his own way. You will have a very special bond with Daniel with all you have gone through to bring him into this world.

The Birth of a True Life Miracle

I feel blessed to have four wonderful sons, and thank God every day for the opportunity to be their father. My previous three children came into this world with relatively no problems and easy childbirths. The first one did have open heart surgery at eighteen months of age, but he recovered well and went on to play football, baseball, and soccer during his youth. He had no limitations growing up, and is now a healthy, strong young adult.

When Daniel, my youngest child, entered this world, he came in with a "bang." He put our faith to the test and stretched it to the extreme. One of the doctors who helped with Daniel's birth told me that there is typically *no recovery* from where his pH levels were at the time of his delivery. He tried to explain to us why Daniel had survived, but couldn't. The only thing he offered was that there were things about babies that simply couldn't be explained. I asked him if he could accept a "miracle." I said that I could. But the doctor had a tough time with it. He seemed to need a medical explanation, one that he could hold on to in scientific terms. The reason *why* Daniel survived was not important to me. What was important, was that he did survive and beat the odds.

June 4

It was 12:10 P.M. in Omaha, Nebraska, and I had just ordered lunch with business associates when my pager went off. My first thought was, oh no, what now? I had not been able to sleep much the night before, due to business problems we were experiencing with a major project, and our biggest customer was about to cancel everything we had worked on during the past eight months. I had just moved my family into a new home, one with plenty of room for the new addition expected mid-July, and everything seemed to be riding on the success of this project.

When I retrieved my page, I was expecting it to be my customer telling us how we had again fallen short. Instead, it was a message from my wife Cathy, telling me that our doctor wanted her to go over to the hospital that morning for additional testing on the baby, and that he was concerned with the check-up results during her regular appointment. Cathy wanted me to arrange, via phone, to have our eight-year-old picked up from school, taken to our house for his baseball gear, then brought to his championship playoff game. She also wanted me to make arrangements for our two-year-old to be picked up from daycare at 6 P.M. She said she had tried to reach my oldest son, who still lived at home with us, to have him help, but had been unable to locate him so far.

I was in a state of shock. It was tough enough dealing with the business problems that I faced, but there is no comparison to the kind of stress that was beginning to take control of my body. I called for Cathy at the doctor's office, but she had already gone over to the hospital. I then asked to talk to Maynard, who was our doctor and close friend, since he always had a reassuring way of addressing our concerns. When Maynard came on the line he said, "David, I'm sorry, but this is very serious," and I immediately felt the color drain from of my face. He then proceeded to tell me that he was concerned for both Cathy and the baby. The baby had a heartbeat, but that was about all. He was totally lifeless and wouldn't respond to probing or anything else they had tried. He said that for Cathy's safety, this baby would have to be taken out within the next three or four days. He also said that the baby didn't have much of a chance to live, and if he did, he would most likely be severely handicapped.

After hanging up the phone, I thought about how blessed I had been to have three healthy boys, born with relatively normal births. This news overwhelmed me. My boss had come over to tell me that my lunch had arrived and that it was getting cold. He took one look at me and knew that I was struggling. I assured him that it was not business-related, and he then asked if Cathy and the baby were all right. I could hardly speak, but went on to tell him of their situation. I felt the need to walk outside for a moment, and told him that I would be back shortly. I walked beyond the parking lot and found some trees to stand under, then completely broke down. I can't recall the last time I cried so passionately. I began praying to God, and asked Jesus to put a strong divine white light around Cathy and the baby, and sent as much healing love as I possibly could to them both.

I have a strong belief that God gives each of us the power to heal. Some find it hard to believe in this power, and most live unaware of this possibility, but I have found that we receive energy from the trees and natural surroundings, and in turn are able to use this energy to heal. It is a complete giving and taking experience. I have also noticed that the beauty of our natural surroundings grows stronger and intensifies with the more energy you give and receive. It is a positive energy force flowing in a loving, healing way, as nature reaches out and supplies us with God-given energy; an energy that is stronger and more powerful than any known drug or man-made substance. I am so thankful that I was made aware of this healing power, as my experience with Daniel put my belief in healing energies to the highest test imaginable.

As the day progressed, it was decided to take Cathy, by ambulance, from our local hospital to St. John's Medical Center in Oxnard, because of their advanced neonatal equipment and specialists. Our doctor thought it would be best to have an emergency C-section to get Daniel out right away. The outlook was not good and they had little hope of Daniel making it at all; and if he did make it he would most likely be severely handicapped.

I caught the first flight home from Omaha and arrived at the airport at 5:30 P.M., right in the heat of rush-hour traffic. I took the coast route and made it to the hospital at 7:20 P.M. Cathy was rolled into the operating room at 8:30 P.M.

When they took Daniel out, he was deep purple and lifeless. As five specialist doctors and four nurses struggled for several minutes to bring life into Daniel, I asked if I could touch him. I reached my hand in and placed it on his leg. I told Daniel to feel the power of God's love and my love come through to his body. I prayed for healing strength to pass through me, into Daniel. At that moment, Daniel opened his eyes for the first time, and looked directly at me. He began to breathe and started his life in this world.

I know that Daniel wouldn't have survived if it wasn't for the great work of the highly-trained professionals who worked on him. But I also know that the power of God's healing love, which passed through me into Daniel at that moment, saved his life. The doctors didn't give Daniel much of a chance of making it through the night, and if he did there were many possible complications. Our son, who was in third grade at the time, asked the next day for his class to pray for Daniel. They started that day and prayed for him many times over the course of the next days and weeks. As little Daniel kept defeating the odds that were against him, prayer groups all over the country were praying for him, while the doctors couldn't explain his miraculous recovery.

One of the nurses who cared for Daniel in the intensive care unit said that in her 27 years in intensive care, she had never seen a baby recover like Daniel. Daniel not only lived, but all body functions began to work normally. As Daniel was taken off the various life-support systems, he began eating on his own, which the doctors didn't feel he would be able to do. He only got stronger and stronger.

After just two weeks, Daniel was allowed to come home from the hospital, even though they originally thought he would need to be there for at least several months. Now, at more than one year of age, Daniel is doing great and is in perfect health.

I know, deep down in my heart, that the power of prayer and love that poured out for Daniel literally saved his life. To all those who showed concern and prayed for Daniel, thank you from the bottom of my heart. Make God, and prayer, a part of each and every day of your life. It can, and does, make a difference.

chapter 10

A Gift of Love

While writing these messages from Jesus, my wife and I celebrated our thirteenth wedding anniversary. The night before, I suddenly realized that I had neglected to get her a present. I attempted to go to bed, but was compelled to write, as is often the case with these "inspired" messages. Many of the words for this book came in the middle of the night, when all I wanted to do was sleep. Now, I have learned to accept and recognize that this is a quiet, peaceful time, with no outside distractions, when the words flow freely. What transpired that night was thirteen "thank you's" to my loving wife, one for each year of marriage. I have included them here, hoping that they can have meaning for you in your own personal relationships as well.

I framed these words of "thank you's" and gave them to my wife the next day. In reply she

A PRAYER OF THIRTEEN THANK YOU'S FOR MY LOVING WIFE

Dear Lord,

1. *Thank you for giving me the ability to experience the warmth of Cathy's love.*
2. *Thank you for the growing and the sharing we have in our relationship.*
3. *Thank you for the seeds of life and children you have given us to bring into this world.*
4. *Thank you for the strength that we are able to pass between one another. When one is down, the other is always there to dust us off and get us back on our feet again.*
5. *Thank you for thirteen years of marriage to someone I learn to love more with each passing year.*
6. *Thank you for giving me a companion who helps bring the light and warmth of your love to each and every day.*
7. *Thank you for the healing we pass between each other in such a glorious and sharing way.*
8. *Thank you for our shared love of doing good in this physical lifetime.*
9. *Thank you for our shared love of natural beauty, and for our love of the outdoors.*
10. *Thank you for our wonderful home.*
11. *Thank you for our willingness to talk openly and honestly together.*
12. *Thank you for the love we share in our incredible children.*
13. *Thank you for the love we share in you.*

Amen

said that this was the greatest present she had ever received. The amount of money we spend on a gift is, many times, what gives us the feeling of how special it is. Only in recent years have I come to realize how much joy is found in simple gifts of love. Last year, my wife asked me what I wanted for Christmas. My reply was, "An evening alone with just the two of us." Now you might say that is not much of a request. But with four boys, quiet times with just the two of us are seldom found and truly cherished.

Jesus is here. Go ahead.

It is important in a marriage to keep creating your love for a spouse, fresh and new with each and every day. Take time to keep blossoming and growing your love together. Too often it is the "hunt" that so captivates you and you are willing to do anything in the name of passion. Once you have achieved your goal and have gained the love of another, you are often guilty of letting your love grow stale. Now that the fun of the chase is over, some of the excitement escapes us.

I did this in my first marriage, and many times put my wife second. I figured she would always be there, so I could spend time on something else. Or, that other things were more important because it related to my business, or the personal pleasures that I so rightfully deserved, and so on and so on.

In contrast, as my second wife and I keep growing together spiritually, our love continues to grow stronger and stronger while we create our love for each other fresh and new. This does not mean that we never disagree and argue, or that we don't get upset with one another. And there are still times I am guilty of withholding my love from her because I'm mad and feel she doesn't deserve it. When I catch myself in these unconscious habits, I realize that I'm only depriving myself, and that I truly enjoy pouring out love towards my wife because I love the way it makes me feel. Isn't it amazing how we will deprive ourselves of sharing love, because we decide another doesn't deserve it?

Jesus is here. Go ahead.

Every time you find yourself depriving yourself of giving out love to another, stop and see how it makes you feel. Remember, all you have to do is change your thoughts at that instant, then create your next thoughts and actions out of love. When you start living this way, you will feel so much better about yourself. Your actions will become contagious, and others around you will respond to you in a much different way.

When you realize that you have the power to create your thoughts and actions anew with every moment, it becomes easier to keep your love fresh and alive. Keep growing together spiritually, and no problem or crisis in your relationship will tear you apart. Give your spouse, and yourself, a "gift of love" each and every day.

chapter 11

"Small Steps"
Rejuvenate Your Soul

The summer before this book was published, while vacationing in Hawaii with my family, I was relaxing by the pool watching my kids laughing and playing in the water, when I suddenly felt this incredible feeling of peacefulness and enjoyment in what I was doing at that exact moment with no outside stress from the "real world." A realization came over me: oftentimes I can't seem to wait for a vacation, getting by day-to-day while waiting for it to arrive. Then it's finally time to go and get away, but I barely stop to take it all in and enjoy it to the fullest while I am there. Once I return home, I think back to how wonderful the vacation was, even though I didn't grasp it completely *while* I was living the experience. I realized while sitting by the pool, that I was too much into the "can't wait" and the "oh, wasn't that great," instead of being fully appreciative and aware of the present moment at hand. I felt inspiration tapping on my shoulder there by the pool, and the following are the thoughts that followed.

Jesus is here. Go ahead.

Many times in your life, you may feel the stress of typical day-to-day pressures that living in this physical world can bring. Stress is greatest when your physical being is not in tune with your soul. It is so easy to get caught up in your physical world; co-workers that drive you crazy, projects with fast-approaching deadlines, or an intimidating boss that makes you fearful. Often you say, if I make this sale or if I achieve this, then the pressure will be off. Once you accomplish this task, you then let the next pressure or new pursuit consume you, and the stress continues to build. If all you are ever after is satisfying your physical needs, you will continue to struggle to satisfy your physical needs. This is because your physical needs just keep growing and growing, and you can never keep pace with them. Many times you get caught up with chasing the dream, so that you never actually take the time to live the dream.

The message that I bring to you today is, to stop right now at this very moment, as you are reading this. Close your eyes, and feel God's presence within you. Let your soul take over your physical body, and just relax. Take a moment to let the warmth of my love warm your soul and feel at complete peace with yourself. When negative thoughts start to enter in, stop and change it at that very moment. You so

often say, but if I had only done this. Forget
that . . . move on; it is time to start fresh,
right now at this moment. Don't worry about
the what if's. Begin each new thought positive-
ly with either "I know" or "I am." If you are
looking for love, give love. If you are looking
for friendship, give friendship. If you are looking for satisfaction, be satisfied. You so often
think you will be satisfied when you get this or
that. Start being satisfied with the pursuit. As
you are striving for something, don't wait for
that something to be completed. Stop, and
enjoy the journey. When you truly believe that
you have eternal life and that this physical existence is just a part of it all, then you start living
each part and each moment. Before you know
it, you begin living your dreams and wishes
with each and every new day.

Even when it appears you are at your dark-
est moment—maybe a loved one has passed on,
or you have lost your job or the love of another—this may be the toughest time for you to
stop and feel God's presence. But I promise, I
will never turn my back on you. I will always
be here. Even when there appears to be no
answers, answers will come. Trust and give
love, unconditional love, and you will receive
love and feel love surround you. It is hard to
feel love, if you close yourself off to love.
Sometimes it takes little steps, which then turn
into big steps, once you let yourself rejoice in
each new small step. When your soul is rejoicing, then you can truly know what living
"heaven on earth" is.

David, you have at times wanted certain
things very badly, and when you didn't get
them you would say, "Okay, even if I don't

understand completely at this moment, I will find the positive in this situation." Then before you knew it, you would be on a new course that turned out to be actually far more fulfilling. If you live your life this way, you can never lose. The strength of God's love will rejuvenate your soul time and time again.

Don't worry about the before and the after. Live your life now, in the present.

chapter 12

Lost Souls

I have often wondered why sometimes I behave in certain ways that seem almost uncharacteristic of me. I sometimes get angry with a greater intensity than I actually felt, and am somewhat baffled by it all upon further reflection. Often we joke about it afterwards, once we have calmed down and are sorry for the outburst, feeling that we must have "been possessed by the devil or something." Well maybe that fancy notion isn't so far off the mark, as this writing session reveals. I know as a child, I was afraid of the dark. It's comforting to know now that darkness has no power over the bright light of God's spirit. Be a mirror and reflect that light into the dark corners of the world.

Jesus is here. Go ahead.

In this message I bring to you, I have already said that you have eternal life. Your soul lives on, and your physical existence here is just a part of your entire life's journey. Know this, for this is so. You live eternally, either in the knowledge of the warmth and love of God, or in darkness. There are many, whom I will call lost souls, who live in darkness. They hang around, not sure where they are or where they are going. They love to find physical beings that show tendencies to the ways in which they, too, lived their physical lives. Remember, there is always comfort in numbers.

That is why, if you don't surround yourself daily with the light of God's great love, it is easy for these souls to intensify your thoughts or desires, which lead you further from your soul and from who you truly want to be. Haven't you ever noticed that you act a certain way in certain situations, without even knowing why you acted this way, or why you responded to a particular person in the way you did? You might have became angry with such an intensity that even you were surprised. Or, you may have rebuked the affection of a loved one because of this or that, when in reality you would have truly enjoyed the warmth of that affection which was being offered.

This is what is known as "evil spirits," or the "devil." These souls aren't really evil, they are just lost. There is no need to fear these souls, for they have no power over you. They are afraid of the light, and will do everything they can to keep you from the warmth and love of God's light. For if you live your life and surround yourself in the warmth and love of God's light each and every day, these souls will either be compelled to step into the light and feel the warmth of God's love, and be instantly reborn into the knowledge and acceptance of God's love, or they will run from it.

chapter 13

Personal Journeys

Two very dear friends of mine had been experiencing trouble in their marriage, and included here is part of their personal journey. When this book was nearly complete, I shared it with both of them, in hopes that it might offer some help during a very difficult time in their lives. The following is what developed during a visit my wife and I had with them.

Jesus is here. Go ahead.

It is mainly up to Ed, if this union of two souls will stay together or move apart. Sara is expanding and breaking down her physical barriers, and her unconscious habits are beginning to fall. There is still one great barrier she needs to overcome to be free, and she will fly like Jonathan Livingston Seagull. She needs to learn the power of healing from within. When she unlocks this passion, she will rejoice in her incredible healing powers, and her dream of being an animal healer will be realized.

It is so very important for Ed and Sara to learn to grow together spiritually, if they are going to keep their souls united and move through this physical lifetime together. This is going to become Sara's life work, and Ed can be a big part of this, for his love of animals is great. But he needs to release the lost soul, who is around him now—the one that influences, or compels, him to have to be perfect in all things.

This soul found Ed many years ago, and has been along for the ride ever since. This soul became so possessed with perfection, that when he passed on from this physical world, he was still so consumed by this perfection that he went right by the light and his angels who were there to greet him. For he felt the light wasn't bright enough, nor did the angels and God look like he thought they should look. He just never opened up to the great warmth and comfort of God's love. He was, and still is, lost in darkness. Ed was perfect for this soul because Ed was developing these same characteristics in his own physical experiences. This soul was delighted to find Ed, and brought on a new intensity to Ed's personality and thought patterns, so much so that Ed doesn't even know why he sometimes acts more strongly than he really wants to.

This is a good time to release this soul, for Ed is finally questioning his actions. Yes, he keeps falling back into his conditioned habits, but he has moments of complete opening. Ed and Sara can work together to release this soul, either into the light and warmth of God's love, or into the darkness—but completely away from Ed. It will have to be a continuing work. Ed and Sara can do it together, or Ed can do it alone, though this is so much harder for a physical being to do. If they are willing to work on this together, it can be a glorious journey for the two of them.

Yes, Cathy has similar traits at times. This is why you and Cathy sometimes seem to be at odds in Ed's presence. There are other souls hanging around as well. They like being near people who already have physical conditions, or conditional habits developed over time, that are similar to theirs. Even though Cathy is very tuned to her soul, her physicality still has conditioned habits that can take over, especially when helped along by a lost soul.

David, it is the same situation when you come in contact with certain people. You feel completely perplexed, and your soul and physical body get completely out of sync. Know that even with as much knowledge as you have gained and opened up to, you still live in a physical world with the ability to have free will. With this wonderful gift comes the ability to develop conditioned habits that aren't necessarily in tune with your soul. This is why you circle yourself, each and every day, with a divine white light. For when you are in the light of God's love, and feeling it with each new thought and action, a soul lost in darkness doesn't stand a chance. That soul will either step into the light, and be reborn into the love and warmth of God's love, or it will run from the light. Continue to circle yourself in the light of God's love daily, and sometimes more often, because there are many lost souls wanting and needing others who believe and act as they do.

chapter 14

In the Beginning—
My First Writings

The following is from one of my very first writings, which occurred several years prior to the moment when Jesus came through my pen and introduced himself directly to me. William was the first of my various teachers to write with me. I felt it might be important to include and note here, that in this writing from William, and the many teachers who came after him, there is a consistency in the messages being passed along through me over the years—a consistency in the inspirations that have reached out to be heard, and have helped me to be open and willing to share with others my experiences of writing with Jesus.

Years ago when William first revealed himself to me, he told me that he'd previously lived on earth during the early 1800s, and prior to that as well. He had a great sense of humor and taught me many things about the afterlife, and how to apply that knowledge to living my life today—all of which paved the way for me to hear the voice of God through Jesus.

Good Morgan—Yes, this is William speaking. Yes, I was from Scandinavia.

You will like the next men who work with you. They are very powerful and will show you more than you could ever know. You will be amazed and will radiate knowledge. Trust and move forward. Don't be afraid. God is with you and with us all, even if you fall. He is always loving and always there. He loves equally, and it doesn't matter what tier you are on. He is there for everyone. You are not better than the next, just because you are on a higher tier. Remember that. Never be better, or think you are better, because you are blessed to have such knowledge. Stay humble and remember love is more important than everything. He will lead the way. He is the light of the world. Follow this light and you will have everlasting life.

Study the Bible. Keep studying. You will learn how it is all connected. People on earth get side-tracked. There are many truths in the Christian teachings, but people don't believe deep down inside. They say they do, but are afraid of the real truth of the Scriptures. The Scriptures were written just as you are writing now. The disciples were inspired by God, and they then wrote the Scriptures. But people get distracted. They all want to be comforted, but not really learn what it means. You are on the right track. Yes, get involved more in the church, learn more how our message is there, the same messages that you are getting, but people get lost and distracted and afraid of the true meanings.

You can show many into the true light. Cathy will help. You are a good teacher. Keep growing spiritually together. This is not nonsense. Why do you think that way? Don't worry, you're always forgiven. You are very hard on yourself. Don't beat yourself up. This gets in your way. Keep it simple. When all is confusing, remember love. Love is the most important thing to share and pass on—a deeper, truer love.

It still is not easy, and doubt is always plentiful in the world. Remember love and trust, above all else, and forgiveness. Don't forget forgiveness. Don't worry, you will learn to understand.

chapter 15

Continuing
Questions and Answers

Over the course of compiling the material for this book, various questions would come to mind, and I would ask Jesus to answer them for me. In this chapter, I have included many of these questions, along with his answers to them.

Jesus is here. Go ahead.

Q. Why did God choose for Jesus to be born in a manger and not in a room at the inn?

Everyone believed, in that day, that a king was royal and had all the riches of the world, and everything was quite lavish. God wanted people to experience the "King of Life" as very humble, and one that didn't need to be put up on a pedestal or throne. The message was to experience things and create your actions from God's love, and by doing so you will have more joy than any material wealth can ever bring you; and, that in eternal life, material wealth means nothing.

Experiencing God's love in everything *is* everything.

Q. If we all have "free will," then how could God choose the manger and dictate what happened?

> Ask and you shall receive. Joseph said, "Father what do I do? Show me a sign," for he did desperately want to stay at the inn. But he had complete faith, and when the option to go to stable arose, he took it.
>
> You all have free will, but know of the presence of a greater intelligence that is God. Ask and you shall receive.

Q. What does "be wise in your own eyes" mean, as you said in our discussion of Proverbs 3 at the beginning of this book? Is not being wise in your eyes showing disrespect and trying to be better than God?

> To "be wise in your own eyes" means to trust the higher intelligence that lives within you, and is a part of you, that which is God. Don't rely on someone else's words, but take it to God in prayer. Take a few minutes each and every day to just be quiet. Clear your mind and spend this time with me, and wonderful thoughts will flow.
>
> When I left this life on earth, I promised to all that, even though I would be gone physically, each of you were filled with the Holy Spirit. This Holy Spirit will teach you all things and

will remind you of everything I have said before. It is for each of you to be aware, and to accept this higher intelligence, which is a part of you. Most are too busy to take the time to listen. Everything else is always more important. You will find, however, that by taking the time to listen, and by opening up to these inspirations, that life is far more fulfilling in every aspect.

Q. What does "fear the Lord" mean, as used in the Bible?

"Never fear the Lord." Love the Lord and embrace the Lord and let his love shine through you.

Q. Then why does the Bible say "fear the Lord?"

The Bible says "never fear the Lord." Writers left out the "never" part. Fear is something that controls people. God doesn't want to control you. He could so easily, if that is what he wanted. However, human beings have this need to control, so henceforth, "fear" appears in this remarkable book. This is one reason why I started writing with you.

Q. I have recently been confronted by individuals who believe this book cannot possibly be direct messages from Jesus. They find there is no fear in these words. There is nothing with which to control people, or keep them in line. Fearing God's wrath is what keeps us on the right path.

Again I ask you, am I getting clear messages from you in this regard?

Yes, you are getting clear messages. There are many like those you have come across, and there have *always* been those who are like that. But know, if this is what they hear from the Bible (which they say are my words), then why did I say at the cross, "Forgive them father, for they know not what they do?" Wouldn't I have said, "Strike these people down, and show your great wrath?" Even Peter, one of my own disciples, became very angry when I said I would be betrayed and crucified. He wanted me to use God's great power to punish those who would do this to me. I then responded in anger towards Peter saying that even though he had been at my side and had heard my own words, how could this still be the image of God he held on to?

There are those who find it easier to hold on to this concept of "if I step out of line, I will be punished." It is much easier for them to feel that they must carry a burden in life. It is more black and white for them that way. To know that God has given us all we will ever need, and with great abundance, makes them have to take responsibility for their own actions. It is much easier for them to have this great higher figure who holds a stick over them saying, "Step out of line, and I will strike you down."

I came and died on the cross to show that this is not the message of God. During my time here, physically and before, people were getting so caught up in condemning those who weren't living the commandments handed down to Moses that they completely lost the message. First of all, they are commitments, not commands. Secondly, man has got to stop judging others around him, and using the Bible as a way to justify it.

The messages in this book are not new. They are what I came and taught when I was here before. I say it again, I could perform one hundred times one hundred miracles, and those who want to see, will, and those who don't will find ways to justify that it is not me. What I offer is just too hard for those to accept.

Take responsibility for your own actions and your own life. Bring God into all things, and be aware of his ever presence. You are already guaranteed everlasting life. Stop saying this person, or that person, doesn't have it right. Stop saying they will be condemned and will receive God's great wrath. Take everything to God in prayer. Feel his answers from deep within, and live a full and abundant life.

Q. So, if there is no "God's wrath," then are there any consequences for our actions?

Absolutely there are consequences for your actions, and we have already discussed this before. Although, having consequences and carrying around guilt and burdens are two different things. To illustrate this point, imagine you have a beautiful vase. You love it, and think it looks great in your house. One day, in anger, you pick up the vase and smash it to the floor. When you finally calm down, you are sorry for your outburst. However, it was not God's wrath that broke the vase because he was angry that you got out of control. The simple truth is, you broke the vase. The consequence of this is, you now no longer have the vase. Likewise, when you lie or cheat, there are all types of consequences that may occur.

Now, there are those who can't believe a vicious criminal could possibly live eternally with God's great warmth and love. They feel it's not fair that they should be equal in the eyes of the Lord. They feel they have lived good, clean lives, and have obeyed all the rules, so they certainly must have more favor with God. If something brings the criminal to the awareness of God's great presence, then yes, he is aware and accepts his life with God and feels the love that God has for everyone. Once you truly feel this presence, then killing another, or lying to another, has no place within your life. You can see how clearly this takes you away from your oneness with God. So, it is not a matter of doing good deeds to win favor with God. It is simply, when you let God become a part of your life and know that he lives within, you do the good deeds because of the great feeling it brings to you.

This is the message that I want you to spread. Don't go out and preach that people are going to be damned if they don't turn to God. Tell them to turn to God and find the great abundance of joy and love it brings to good times, and also the great strength it brings in difficult times. Spread the great news of the cross, and know that you can live eternally with God.

Q. There are also those who say Christians will be asked to bear burdens and suffer for their beliefs. That through this suffering we grow stronger and will be the better for it. Can you help me understand this?

As I have already said, be willing to put aside material wealth, monetary satisfaction, or instant gratification if it interferes with finding oneness with God. This does not mean don't enjoy abundance in life. It is also not necessary to carry around burdens and guilt to be faithful.

I died on the cross to show that there is more to life than the here and now; life is eternal. There is no need to carry guilt around, and there is no God's wrath for whatever sins or actions you have done. How can one say, "We must carry the burden of the cross?" I died on the cross not to make you feel guilty, but to show that you have eternal life with an all-loving and all-forgiving God. Rejoice in the cross, and in the message it brings.

Q. Why did you choose Matthew and the others to be disciples?

Matthew was living an unconscious life, away from God's love. When he heard me speak, he was enthralled, and his life, for the first time, had meaning. He started to enjoy his experience here on earth and wanted to follow me and learn more. He was a natural-born teacher, and he couldn't help but tell others. He was a wonderful storyteller, and it gave him great joy to spread the word. Each of the disciples were different, but similar in their willingness to open up themselves to this teaching and to pass it on.

Q. Why did you perform so many miracles?

To show the power of God's love, and that each and every one of you can have this. This is what so many miss in my message. I am a teacher, and if you truly listen, I teach that you too can perform miracles.

Q. In my earlier writings, I was told about tiers, or planes. What does this mean, and was I getting a clear message from my teacher at that time?

What do you think? Is the message not the same basic message that I bring to you today? It is true that you and I have not talked about planes or tiers before, and this is because you have never asked; it is not something of great importance in the messages I have passed on through you.

Planes, or tiers (one and the same), are not what you might think. Souls don't live separately on different tiers. This is just a way your teacher was presenting, to you, the ability a soul has to experience life here on earth with the knowledge and openness to communicate with those not in the physical world. When a soul on earth is on a higher tier, this does not mean they are better than another soul. They are, however, able to accomplish much more, because they are more in tune to the spiritual world, and to the great energy and power this brings to your everyday living experiences.

You have already said, in the beginning of this book, that you are able to live a more conscious life, and that you create your actions from this knowledge of God's love. To relate it to tennis, which is something you enjoy playing, there are 3.5-rated players and there are 6.5-rated players. A 6.5 player has an easier time grasping certain aspects of the game, concepts that a 3.5 player can't even comprehend. It doesn't mean the 6.5 player is a better person than the other, it only means that they can achieve more, within that sport.

The first, second, and third tiers are the same. I came to earth in the fourth tier, with complete knowledge of who I was, where I came from, and with direct access and open communication with God, the Father.

Q. Are you God?

Yes, but God is hard for you to completely grasp. The best way to understand who God is, is by understanding God the Father, Son, and Holy Ghost. He is all things. You are all a part of God experiencing life, each with individual souls. I am different because I am God; the Son and Father are One.

I am different only in a way words don't do justice, since you also are a part of God. The difference is, I was created not through two physical beings; not conceived by a man and a woman. I was conceived completely by God. You were conceived by a man and a woman, who were created by God. I am different, because of the process that I came into physical form. When you speak to me, you are speaking to God. When you speak to another soul, such as Ralph, you are speaking to a soul who is a *part* of God, but who is not *all* of God. God is the whole, and is all there is.

Q. Is there a Satan?

There is no one soul who is as powerful as God, and is struggling for your soul. So, if you are asking me, "Is there one superior evil spirit?" no. But, as I have said before, there are what you would call "evil spirits"—those who are lost in darkness. Remember, God gave everyone a mind, and the power to choose their actions. These "evil spirits" are clever enough to affect and flow into your thinking patterns. This is why you must always circle yourself with the divine white light of God's love. They are afraid of the light, and nothing is more powerful than God. If they are lucky enough to experience the light and feel the warmth of God's love, they are then enlightened and are able to walk into the light, for God never turns his back on even one soul.

Q. Why does fear grip us with such a firm hold? I've been writing with you for some time, yet fear is still a part of my life.

Fear in the physical world is plentiful. Don't beat yourself up so much. You are now open to know when you are acting out of fear. In the past, you lived without any of this knowledge. Have you not said in your own words "that your experiences are more fulfilling since you have opened yourself up to these truths you've been receiving"? You still have complete free will, and you still have conditioned responses that grip you from time to time. Rejoice in the fact that you are aware and conscious of these experiences being generated out of fear. Simply stop and surround yourself with love, and create new thoughts and new actions. The more you do this, the less fear will be a part of your actions.

It's just like when you are teaching Cathy tennis. She is now aware of mistakes that she makes and she is working towards creating her actions on the tennis court so those conditioned habits that she has built up over time interfere less and less in her journey towards playing better tennis.

This is the same in your learning to live as I did. Remember, even I, when here in physical form, had to deal with fear and anger, for I, too, was free to experience all. I felt pain and I felt happiness. Keep committing yourself to being truthful in all experiences. Not because I will condemn you if you are not, but know that by living this way, you free your soul to being who it truly wants to be. Remember, don't go for momentary satisfaction, but strive for everlasting satisfaction.

Q. I have some concern that thoughts and concepts, which I have been learning in recent months, might be influencing my writings with you. Even though the majority of this book is finished, I wonder if more of my thoughts are now filtering into the messages?

You are concerned that what you have recently learned in your studies is coming into these writings and that you've turned them into my (your) words. I brought these messages to you, just as I have brought it to others. If sometimes they seem the same as something else, then be elated; don't question. Inspiration is all around you; sometimes it comes in the form of another person's words, or sometimes from the wind. Don't discount either source. When you feel it deep within your soul, you know it to be true. It is okay to edit my words, for my words come through you. Sometimes they come through so pure that they don't need to be touched; but other times the message will come, and for whatever reason, they are not grammatically perfect. This does not mean the message is any less important. If there are areas you doubt and don't know if your editing changes the meaning, ask and you shall receive the answers.

Q. What about the Buddhists and Muslims and all the other religions? Will they have eternal life, or do they have it all wrong?

As I said to you when writing on the Bible and being inspired to write this message for today, you first had to study the Bible, so we weren't having a one-sided conversation. Study and learn what is written and taught within other religions, as you did here. Then we will have a wonderful conversation that you can, in turn, pass on to others.

Q. So, may I assume there will be further books and messages that you will continue to pass along through my pen?

Absolutely. Why would I stop? It is for you to decide. Each day that you evolve, more questions and new situations arise. You have already asked where do all the different religions play a part in the greater whole. You already know that there is only one God, so how is God a part of all religions? This is a book in itself. Get this first message out now, and as this message opens up awareness for those who read these words, you will already be writing and studying as the next book evolves. There also will be further books of the Bible to explore and cross-reference. Get this first message out and know that there will be more to come.

Believe in yourself. Believe in these messages. Believe in my help.

chapter 16

An Open Dialogue

When the messages for this book seemed almost complete, I began sharing the manuscript with my immediate family and a few others. At this point, no one other than my wife and children knew anything about it. Included in this chapter are the initial responses, which I now refer to as "an open dialogue." It is my viewpoint that to grow spiritually, we need to openly discuss our beliefs with others. This is not so we can preach to others that we have all the answers; but, to truly understand what we believe, we need to be able to express these beliefs openly and honestly.

The first response I received was a letter from a family member. He has been married for the past thirty-three years and has three grown children, one of which is newly married and attending seminary. At first I was taken aback with his words, and braced myself for what else might be forthcoming. Then I took a moment to step aside, and allowed Jesus to come through to truly inspire me. It was his inspirations that helped me reply to that initial letter.

After I received that first response, I encouraged others who had read the manuscript, to also put their feelings and thoughts down on paper. The next letter I received was from my wife's mother. Again, I didn't know how she felt about the manuscript until I read her words. These letters became the catalyst for adding this chapter. In reading this chapter, you will find that even family members don't necessarily agree with each other regarding the messages in this book. However, we can all benefit from these thought-provoking questions and conversations that have taken place.

What I have learned is, whether or not you find your own truth in this book, it is important and useful in that it helps each of us discover what we truly believe. It forces us to think for ourselves, and to not just take for granted that which we have been told or taught. It makes us recognize and evaluate our beliefs, and helps get us off "autopilot" by making us think deeper for ourselves.

It has begun: "an open dialogue". . .

The Initial Letter Received

It was my original intent, to begin this dialogue with my first official response to the manuscript. Initially, this family member considered having his letter printed in this book. After some additional thought, he said that since he disagreed with my "theology," he no longer would allow it to be included. I let him know that I would respect his wishes, even though I thought it was a great opportunity for him to express his personal opinions, since there were many areas of the book that he disagreed with.

It is my feeling that his concerns and areas of disagreement are to be expected by many of those who read this book. I, myself, have over the years questioned some of these same things. The answers I have found are expressed in my response to him, and I feel it's important to include them in this chapter. It is for these reasons, that I will attempt to outline below an overview of his viewpoints and concerns. Know that there is great love shared between us, and I believe that the basis for his letter to me was out of that love.

To begin with, he felt strongly that what was presented in this book was not true Christian doctrine or belief, and that nowhere in the Bible, Christian writings, or tradition, were the concepts of reincarnation and tiers advocated or preached. He directed me to Acts: 2, and felt that God had spoken directly to a few chosen people like Moses, who in turn delivered God's message to the masses; and at Pentecost, the Holy Spirit was given to us as a counselor and guide, and it was our responsibility, as believers in Christ, to stay in touch with God through prayer to the Holy Spirit. He warned me against rewriting scripture, and directed me to Revelation 22:18-19 (NIV), which states,

> 18 I warn anyone who hears the words of the prophecy of this book: If anyone adds anything to them, God will add to him the plagues described in this book.
>
> 19 And if anyone takes words away from this book of prophecy, God will take away from him his share in the tree of life . . .

He had just finished a year-long study of Revelation, and personally did not want to be on the wrong side of God when the times described there were played out. Finally, he directed me to 2 Corinthians 11:14-15 (NIV), which reads,

> 14 And no wonder, for Satan himself masquerades as an angel of light.
>
> 15 It is not surprising, then, if his servants masquerade as servants of righteousness.

My Letter in Response

I have read your letter and know the love and concern you have, and I am grateful for that. I also appreciate the time you have taken; one, to read the manuscript, and two, to discuss your thoughts openly with me. I may have learned more about your beliefs in this short letter than I have in the thirty-four years you have been a part of my life. I feel open communication is vital to expanding and learning who we are and who we want to be. Christ came and taught of God's great love, and showed us by how he lived that making choices and actions from love is the greatest gift God has created—unselfish, unconditional love. If this manuscript has started communication and open discussion, then it already has been worth the experience of sharing it with you.

I have always had a great deal of respect and admiration for your marriage and the love you both share, and for the incredible kids you have raised. When I was struggling in my first marriage, I wished I could have what it appears you have. First, a great friendship; second, great faith; and third, continual growth together with a love that radiates stronger with each passing year. I have found this my second time around.

I can't reply to your mention of the Hindu beliefs, because, quite frankly, I haven't yet studied them; so I don't know enough about the Hindu faith to comment. As for hippies and flower people, I again don't feel I know enough about what was brought here, in the 60s and 70s, of the Eastern religions. But, I promise you, I plan to keep expanding and learning, and some day I hope I can make intelligent statements on these various religions and beliefs.

At this time, I will only address the issues of reincarnation and planes, or tiers, from the perspective of what I have learned from my communication with Jesus, or the Holy Spirit, as I believe they are one and the same.

First, I believe Jesus came to this earth to show us that death does not have a hold over us; that we have eternal life. Our soul lives on; only our physical body perishes. We have eternal life in the light and warmth of God's love, if we choose to. I believe you feel the same on this. Whether you believe a soul lives on only in heaven, or here on earth, I know you believe a soul lives on. The Bible, however, does address the issue of whether a soul might reappear here on earth again, in the Book of Matthew. I have read four different translations of the Bible and it has appeared in each version. I will quote King James version, Matthew 17:3-13, which reads;

3 And behold, there appeared unto them Moses and Elias talking with him.

4 Then answered Peter, and said unto Jesus, Lord, it is good for us to be here: if thou wilt, let us make here three tabernacles; one for thee, and one for Moses, and one for Elias.

5 While he yet spake, behold, a bright cloud overshadowed them: and behold a voice out of the cloud, which said, This is my beloved Son, in whom I am well pleased; hear ye him.

6 And when the disciples heard *it*, They fell on their face, and were sore afraid.

7 And Jesus came and touched them, and said, "Arise, and be not afraid."

8 And when they had lifted up their eyes, they saw no man, save Jesus only.

9 And as they came down from the mountain, Jesus charged them, saying, "Tell the vision to no man, until the Son of man be risen again from the dead."

10 And his disciples asked him, saying, "Why then say the scribes that Elias must first come?"

11 And Jesus answered and said unto them, "Elias truly shall first come, and restore all things.

12 But I say unto you, that Elias is come already, and they knew him not, but have done unto him whatsoever they listed. Likewise shall also the Son of man suffer of them."

13 Then the disciples understood that he spake unto them of John the Baptist.

In The Living Bible version, I feel it is easier to read Matthew 17:10-13;

10   His disciples asked, "Why do the Jewish leaders insist Elijah must return before the Messiah comes?"

11   Jesus replied, "They are right. Elijah must come and set everything in order.

12   And, in fact, he has already come, but he wasn't recognized, and was badly mistreated by many. And I, the Messiah, shall also suffer at their hands."

13   Then the disciples realized he was speaking of John the Baptist.

As for tiers or planes, I would have quoted my Father's words to you, "The floor is level at the foot of the cross," for I believe this thoroughly, and it appears you do as well, for you have already quoted his words. I will however, quote my book, page 116:

He loves equally, and it doesn't matter what tier you are on. He is there for everyone. You are not better than the next, just because you are on a higher tier. Remember that. Never be better, or think you are better, because you are blessed to have such knowledge. Stay humble and remember love is more important than everything. He will lead the way. He is the light of the world. Follow this light and you will have everlasting life.

And from page 126 of this book:

Planes, or tiers (one and the same), are not what you might think. Souls don't live separately on different tiers. This is just a way your teacher was presenting to you, the ability a soul has to experience life here on earth with the knowledge and openness to communicate with those not in the physical world. When a soul on earth is on a higher tier, this does not mean they are better than another soul. They are, however, able to accomplish much more, because they are more in tuned to the spiritual world, and to the great energy and power this brings to your everyday living experiences.

You have already said in the beginning of this book, that you are able to live a more conscious life, and that you create your actions from this knowledge of God's love. To relate it to tennis, which is something you enjoy playing, there are 3.5-rated players and there are 6.5-rated players. A 6.5 player has an easier time grasping certain aspects of the game, concepts that a 3.5 player can't even comprehend. It doesn't mean the 6.5 player is a better person than the other, it only means that they can achieve more, within that sport.

The first, second, and third tier are the same. I came to earth in the fourth tier, with complete knowledge of who I was, where I came from, and with direct access and open communication with God, the Father.

I know you have more concerns, and as you said, you "will only mention a few" at this time. I sincerely hope we can keep this open dialogue going, for I, too, feel there is more we can discuss.

In closing, and this is the area where possibly our beliefs may differ greatly, I believe there is only one God, and that there is no force, evil spirit, or Satan that is more powerful than the love of God. I don't believe that there are two equal forces struggling for my soul. I believe that when you accept God's love and make it a part of your everyday living experience, a Satan, or an evil force, wouldn't stand a chance. So, I ask you to re-read the manuscript, and as you read it, ask yourself, do these words bring you closer to knowing and feeling

God's love, or does it take you further from it? Do living the principles that these words speak bring greater joy and meaning to your life? If after you have done this, you still feel that it is truly Satan masquerading as the light of the world, then please keep praying to the Holy Spirit and having these open discussions with me. For I don't find that your words are "mean or harsh." And I agree that the Holy Spirit is telling you to "get it out" and to openly, with love in your heart, discuss these concerns you have brought forth.

I will close this letter as I began, in that I am grateful for your love and concern. I will continue to pray to the Lord and ask for his guidance to determine what future direction I should take, and will make him a part of all that I do.

Sincerely,
Dave

The Second Letter Received

The next letter I received was from my mother-in-law. You can imagine how I opened this letter with trepidation, not knowing how she would respond, especially after receiving that first one. After reading her moving letter, I didn't feel a need to write back. I just wiped the tears from my eyes and said, "Thank you," from the bottom of my heart.

Dear Dave,

I find it difficult to put my thoughts on paper, but I will try. From first grade through high school, I was taught a religion that was based on fear rather than love. I don't know why, but sometime in my early twenties I started to have a problem accepting the things I had been taught all those years. I *lost* my faith, and instead of probing or looking into other religions, I just *dropped out*.

I attempted to raise my children in the faith, but after awhile just stopped. I felt it would be better for them to be able to "choose" their own beliefs when they were adults. Therefore, even though we had a loving family, there was no formal religious teachings.

From time-to-time over the years I have given some thought to finding some spiritual guidance, but I guess I was too burned out from my early teachings to really do anything about it. This does not mean I gave up on my belief of God (or for a time I called it a "Higher Power"). I always prayed directly to him, but not on a regular basis. It seems I only prayed when I wanted or needed something badly, and I'm sad to say that I don't think my prayers were answered.

This is why I feel extremely "blessed" to have the opportunity to read this book. There is *so* much to try to learn and retain. But the basic message that keeps coming back to me is:

God is not to be *feared*.
God loves all of us *unconditionally*.
We all have a *free will* and we make our own *choices*.
Joy will come from loving and doing good for others.

This book has been written with great inspiration, love, and faith. It is very easy to read and understand. I believe it will be a controversial book, but it will make some people actually start *thinking*, rather than just trusting what they have been taught. For those with "open" minds, it will bring great joy and peace. But as it says in this book, take from it that which is good for you and leave the rest. After all, we do have free choice.

Thank you David (and Cathy) for making it possible for

me to "believe" again. I have a long way to go and much study to do, but every journey begins with a first step.

I Will Love You Forever,
Mom Shaw

The Next Letter Received

This third letter was from one of my friends whom I spoke of in the "Personal Journeys" chapter of this book. As mentioned there, she and her husband had shared some of the difficulties that they were experiencing in their relationship with my wife and I while we were visiting them. We gave our love and support to both, and shared the manuscript for this book with them. This letter in many ways confirmed to me that the messages in this book have value and meaning to others.

Aloha Dave,

It was such a treat to see both you and Cathy again after many years, and a true joy to meet three of those beautiful boys who make your lives so enriched. I was also very glad that Alice made the trip despite her fears, as I feel Kauai is a great place to heal, and I know it was good for her. Your life has certainly taken a major detour in such an extraordinary way. I know you must still pinch yourself to see if you are awake and really experiencing all of this.

When Ed told me what you had been doing, I must admit I wasn't shocked or surprised; only interested in the how and why. It was tremendous having you here to share your experiences personally with us, and I must also tell you how incredible it was to receive the healing that came my way. I, too, have been on a different path these last few months, trying to get in touch with my soul and find out what makes me tick. I've been Sara, Ed's wife, for so many years, that I've somewhat lost my identity and purpose. Now the time has come for me to find myself again.

I have had an interesting journey getting here, with pain, doubt, guilt, and indecisiveness all coming into play. But, I truly believe God has helped me choose the right path by sending different people my way to help in many areas. I'm so grateful for all these beings—both in human and spirit forms. I now have a clearer understanding of what I should do and what I want to do; and this is to somehow bring healing to both animals and humans—all life forms, really.

It wasn't surprising to read your manuscript and find so much reference to love, and to see how healing is so connected to this. The repeated notion is that all things must come from a love base, which in turn brings clarity and happiness to your life. It's really such a simple concept—one we've all heard countless times before. But, to hear it or see it written through Jesus' words during this century, makes it much more relevant and meaningful, and *essential*.

It's very exciting that your writings encourage everyone to heal and use the universal life force, or energy, that is available to all of us. We need only to channel it and put it to good use through love. As you now know, I've been exposed to healers throughout my life, and have seen many miracles, having been the recipient of both instant and long-term healing. Over the years, the life force has always been there for me through the spirit world, and I've had many occasions to call on the guides for help. However, my most consistent reaction and concern to this has been doubt—that word that you use many times as well. It seems too good to be true: "Ask and you shall receive." It can't be this easy. Why should it happen to me? How can I heal? Doubt, as you reminded me, is a part of fear. Fear is negative and self-defeating, and must somehow block the energy, life force, or whatever you want to call it.

I am now practicing my newfound desire to be confident and positive, and to know that only good can happen if you heal out of love and ask for help from God and our guides in the spirit world. I've also been fortunate enough to incorporate some Reiki, which is helping me prepare my mind (which is always so full of other stuff!). Visualization of healthy tissue and of the divine white healing light, plus listening to your inner intuition and to your hands; it's all there, if we can just take the time to practice and perform these acts through love and compassion.

This is an exciting time and I'm grateful to have had your encouragement and confirmation that it is possible, and that it is happening. To have experienced the healing through you, without you even knowing it was needed, is still so clear in my mind. When you were showing me how you were healing Ed, you put your hands on my elbow and I felt such warmth and energy. It was almost like a "lovers touch" (that's the only way I can explain the chemistry!). At that moment, I stopped listening and made a mental note to ask you to touch my hip later, to perhaps get relief from the pinched nerve I'd had for several months. I then refocused on what you were saying, and later didn't remember to ask you for that healing.

Early the next morning (3 A.M.), I awoke to hear a cat caught in the trap by the front door. I jumped out of bed to check on this, and realized, in my sleepy haze, that I didn't have any pain in my hip; it felt perfect—no ache, or the acute shooting pain I'd been experiencing for some months. Then I remembered our healing discussion, and realized what had happened. Just by thinking about my hip, I am sure that I directed the healing energy from your hands to my hip. I have no other explanation and believe you concur that this is what happened. What a blessing, and miracle, to boost my trust and belief in what is happening to us both!

So, no more doubt; it's time to act and to trust that people or animals who need me, and are receptive, will come my way. I've been on the receiving end of these healing miracles for many years. It's now time to give back and help others in a real way.

Thank you for sharing your story with us and for caring so much that you put yourselves on the line to help Ed and me through this difficult time. I'm not afraid, as I know this is all part of God's plan, and I'm leaving the relationship in his hands. I can trust him. You too have a few more challenges to overcome as you continue on this path of getting your manuscript published. But if it touches many people the way it did me, the knowledge and love will only snowball and get people thinking and talking.

I wish you continued inspiration and perseverance in your beliefs, and that the writings will continue to flow like a fountain of water. God Bless you both on your mission.

Much love and Aloha,
Sara

P.S. The following are some specific questions I'd like you to ask.

Questions from Sara

On authenticity/proof:

Q. I hate to even bring this up, as it's actually not something I really have to know, but I'm finding that other people want proof, or substantiation, that it's really "Jesus" speaking or writing through you, and not just another good or well-meaning spirit. According to friends of mine, who are Jehovah's Witnesses, the Bible says that when a person dies, their spirit moves on and does not, or cannot, communicate with the living. Those that do are evil spirits; so they don't believe Jesus would communicate with the living from a biblical point of view. I personally believe this is incorrect, but I don't know the Bible well enough. What can I say to them and others who don't want to consider that this communication is possible?

Jesus is here. Go ahead.

Sara, you have such a loving heart and it is a joy to experience life through your eyes. As you have mentioned in your question, it isn't really important if this message is from me, or from just another good spirit. I could perform one hundred times one hundred miracles, and people would still question. Look what happened when I actually lived in a physical body and lived on earth. There is never proof enough for doubters.

But, what I feel is important to address is this concept that an evil spirit is possibly passing on these messages, as described by your friend who is a Jehovah's Witness. Have them read the words of this book and find for themselves if living the principles I pass through Dave bring them closer to God, or further from God. Do living these principles bring joy to your soul, or great sorrow? When at times it seems confusing and different messages are contradicting, then always go to the simple meanings of the words. Do these words bring you closer to knowing and experiencing love in your life, or do they take you to a dark and evil place? God is love. Always ask God to be a part of your thoughts and actions. Don't rely on what others say a certain passage in the Bible means. Open yourself up (which you are doing) to experiencing God's love and warmth in all things. Ask and you shall receive.

There is so much proof that angels and good spirits communicate daily with those in the physical world. Remember, I came and proved that we have eternal life; yet there are still those who won't, or don't, want to believe. They want to see it right before their very own eyes. My answer to this is, open your eyes and you will see. You either believe in me, or you don't. If fear is your guide and leader, it is very hard to experience all of God's greatness. But, I say to you, he is available to everyone. If you trust, you will see.

On the healing of others (if they don't believe or don't want to be):

Q. This is important to me, as I'd like to help a few people; one in particular, who is stuck in a very negative and sad life with pain, both physically (broken bones in foot), and emotionally (two broken marriages, leaving him broken and broke). I suggested healing, but I don't think he either wants it, or can accept the thought that it might help. He's stuck! I do believe that when you're open and receptive, incredible things can and do happen. However, can healing be effective if the person is blocking the idea? I guess this is where animals will be a great learning experience for me!

Jesus is here. Go ahead.

Healing those who don't believe is difficult. They let their own doubts and fears block the passage and flow of energy. You felt Dave's healing touch because you were in tune with it. You describe it as a "lover's touch," and that is exactly what it is. An enormous amount of love passing through, which is the most powerful healing that God has created. You must learn this in your own healings which you will perform. Let your passion flow, and those you are healing will feel the warmth and love in your hands. Don't be inhibited; let the intensity glow and radiate.

Now, I have said it is difficult to heal someone who is not receptive to this most powerful form of healing. Two things happen that can block the flow. Their thought process, and your own. When you have thoughts of doubt and uncertainty, take a moment to feel my presence, and then go on. In the work you will do with animals, you will find them very receptive to your loving touch.

You can't force someone to accept this loving touch. Remember, you all have been given free will to make your own choices. As for your friend, keep passing healing love to him each and every day. When you are in his physical presence, hold his hands and pass love through. Show him you care. Bit by bit, his barriers might fall, and, then again, they might not.

Remember, life is a constant giving and receiving. Keep pouring your love and healing out unconditionally. That is, don't put conditions on your healing (such as, you have to see immediate results or you will stop). Enjoy the process. Dave has these same questions; why at some times miracle healings take place, and at other times it seems as though nothing has taken place. Dave has learned to trust, to keep giving out healing love, and he has had some remarkable results. But at times it seems as if nothing has transpired. He has learned to go on and say, "what have I got to lose, when there is so much to gain."

The feeling you receive when the healing process is taking place is joyous. You are giving to another. Open yourself up to how incredible the feeling is to freely give, and you will rejoice in what you receive.

Your friend is locked in pain and is unconsciously holding on to it.

A Letter In Closing

The final letter that I share with you is one from my brother. His influence on my life is far greater than he will ever know. He is gifted in so many areas, but above all, he is the most caring and giving person I know. This letter has given me great strength in times when I have fallen prey to questioning and doubts of my own. His letter voices many of the same concerns that I have had about myself.

When David first mentioned that he had written a book, there was a certain tension in his mannerism, and he was clearly tentative about disclosing the full nature of this undertaking. I soon learned why, and immediately had mixed emotions of my own. What David, my brother and probably closest friend in the world, revealed to me was certainly perplexing, maybe catastrophic, perhaps miraculous, or simply just unbelievable. In some ways, what David had brought to light both challenged my beliefs and knowledge of Judeo-Christian truths, and, in other ways, also confirmed them.

This book has ignited a dialogue in our family that has been both challenging and refreshing. Without a doubt, it has sparked serious concern, continuing debate, deep questioning, and an ample amount of prayer. This family is one in which Christ plays a central role. Our father was a Navy chaplain, my nephew and niece-in-law are currently in seminary. My mother and I are elders in the Presbyterian Church, and both of my sisters are deeply involved in the church and with its mission work.

None of us were prepared for the "bomb" David dropped when he revealed the first few chapters of rough manuscript. Our first reactions were of deep concern. There can be nothing more important than one's eternal soul, and an unforgivable sin mentioned in the New Testament is blasphemy against the Holy Spirit. Some in our family had thoughts that David had crossed the line, and that what he was doing could not be consistent with the word of God as we currently understood it.

David is more than a brother to me; he is my closest male friend and it would be difficult to love a brother more. After he presented us with this material, I found myself, along with the rest of our family, considering several possibilities:

1) David had gone crazy;
2) he was possessed by a demon or the Devil himself;
3) he was involved in spiritual warfare and was probably losing;
4) he was a cunning and calculating opportunist cashing in on the millennium craziness;
5) he was misguided and perhaps expressing suppressed feelings or beliefs;

6)   or, perhaps, he was in touch with the living Christ in a manner unknown to us before.

Option one: David had gone crazy. Considering this is somewhat tempting, in that he's my younger brother and all. But seriously, by observing David's own lucidity and questioning over this matter, combined with his overall rational behavior in all other aspects of his life, I am lead to believe that this is not a likely conclusion.

Option two: David is possessed by a demon or the Devil himself. This option will probably occur as likely to many, especially to the most conservative Christians. Although personally, I cannot buy this assumption based on the same rationale that Jesus used when confronted and accused of, himself, using the power of Satan to perform his miracles. Jesus, in his reply, was straightforward and logical; a house cannot stand that is divided against itself. Not only are the messages of love in this book consistent with Christ's teachings, but David clearly conveys that Jesus Christ is his Lord and Savior. This stands up to the tests provided for us in 1 John 4 (NIV) (particularly verses 15-18):

15   If anyone acknowledges that Jesus is the Son of God, God lives in him and he in God.

16   And so we know and rely on the love God has for us.
God is love. Whoever lives in love lives in God, and God in him.

17   In this way, love is made complete among us so that we will have confidence on the day of judgment, because in this world we are like him.

18   There is no fear in love. But perfect love drives out fear, because fear has to do with

punishment. The one who fears is not
made perfect in love.

Option three: David is involved in spiritual warfare.
Quite possibly this could be the case, and I believe
there are many devoted Christians that see this within
their own lives. This suggests two forces at work, Christ
and Satan. The Bible teaches us several things here;
one is that Christ is more powerful than any adversary.
It also teaches us to pray for deliverance, that the Lord
is faithful and will protect us from the evil one (2
Thessalonians 3:2,3)(NIV).

2   And pray that we may be delivered from
     wicked and evil men, for not everyone has
     faith.
3   But the Lord is faithful, and he will strength-
     en and protect you from the evil one.

Additionally, it teaches us to pray for wisdom and
that God will answer our prayers when we have faith
(James 1:5,6 NIV).

5   If any of you lacks wisdom, he should ask
     God, who gives generously to all without
     finding fault, and it will be given to him.
6   But when he asks, he must believe and not
     doubt, because he who doubts is like a wave
     of the sea, blown and tossed by the wind.

So, while there may be some aspect of spiritual warfare at work here, I feel we should not be frozen in fear,
but rather put our trust in God. I feel confident that truth
will prevail if we are willing to lift this in prayer to God
and listen patiently for his answer.

Option four: David is a cunning and calculating opportunist looking to cash in on the millennium madness.

While many who do not know David, and perhaps some who do, will jump to this conclusion, this is one alternative I completely discount. Anyone who loves Jesus as David does, and believes in his messages so completely, would not risk his eternal soul for so temporary a gain as this.

Option five: David is simply misguided and perhaps expressing suppressed feelings or beliefs. This alternative is probably the most compelling one for the agnostics or atheists. Perhaps the whole premise of religion is false, and Karl Marx's communist viewpoint was right when he said, "Religion is the opiate of the masses." For me, this alternative would be extremely devastating if it were true, because it would undermine my entire belief system. However, too much has been revealed to me in my life to abandon Christ as my own Lord and Savior. An interesting point here is that David is both directly and indirectly responsible for leading me, more than five years ago, to a deeper and more complete commitment to Jesus Christ. I have personally witnessed miracles in my life that would probably take a book of their own to cover properly. So, I must conclude that if David is just a poor, misguided soul, then I am in the same boat too, and my entire life experience has been a mere illusion.

Option six: Perhaps David is in touch with the living Christ in a manner unknown to us before. Christ taught his disciples that the Kingdom of God is spiritual in nature. He also taught that the Kingdom of God is within us. The Jews of Jesus' time were not expecting a messiah that would come in the form of Jesus of Nazareth. They were expecting a conquering hero. It also appears that the disciples, who spent countless hours walking and talking with Jesus, did not at first understand what he was saying and revealing to them regarding the kingdom of God. Their first reaction to his death on the cross was one of denial, fear, and defeat. However, when they witnessed their risen Lord, they finally gained an understanding that helped them to go forward, thereby changing the world forever.

It would be arrogant to assume that we can understand, completely, all that God has intended for us. We know however, that he did promise us a counselor, and Christ followed this promise with these words in John 16:12-15 (NIV) which read;

12　"I have much more to say to you, more than you can now bear.

13　But when he, the Spirit of truth, comes, he will guide you into all truth. He will not speak on his own; he will speak only what he hears, and he will tell you what is yet to come.

14　He will bring glory to me by taking from what is mine and making it known to you.

15　All that belongs to the Father is mine. That is why I said the Spirit will take from what is mine and make it known to you."

As is noted throughout the Bible, God continually used imperfect men to help fulfill his purpose on earth. The disciples themselves were an example of ordinary men made extraordinary through the power of the living Christ. David is not trying to preach a new religion. He is merely attempting to share a profound phenomenon that he has experienced within his own life, hoping that it will further God's purpose and allow God's love to shine through. We still need to open our own hearts, pray for wisdom, and listen for the answers God provides.

Doug Austin

chapter 17

On the Seventh Day He Rested

Jesus is here. Go ahead.

In the Book of Genesis, it says that God created the earth in six days, and on the seventh day he rested. Many of you really took this to heart—that God finished creating after seven days. . .

God has never stopped creating.

In every new blossom that blooms, God is creating.

With every new baby born, God is creating.

Each thought you have, every action you take, God is creating.

In every moment of every day, God is creating.

The days, as mentioned in Genesis, are not within a space of time that you recognize as a twenty-four-hour period. Hundreds and thousands of years were a part of each segment of time mentioned here. Evolution is not proof that God does not exist. Evolution is proof that God does exist. Evolution is constantly taking place, as God continues to create.

There are those who feel that when God

rested on the seventh day, he was done and now stays in a state of rest. God's work is never done. He is creating every day, every moment—through you. With first your thought, then your action.

Know this to be true, and create the eighth day in the knowledge of his love. Live consciously of all decisions you make which, in turn, shape your life. Feel God's presence in all things, and truly experience "heaven on earth."

chapter 18

Christ, My Lord and Savior

Jesus is here. Go ahead.

Imagine God creating man to physically experience all that is. God freely communicating with physical man, and man freely communicating with God; the source of all that is.

As evolution kept evolving moment to moment, mankind forgot their oneness with the creator, and as they turned away from God, they used God, or who they said God was, to control one another. The more separated man became from his source, the more controlling and condemning of each other he became. As the laws of life that were passed through to mankind became instruments to condemn and slipped further from the truth of living them, God created Jesus, who taught the evolving physical universe the simple truths of God. Jesus taught how each and every one was connected and a part of God; that life was far more than physical. He showed that just by knowing this and becoming aware of God's magnificent presence, we could bring about a life far more fulfilling and far more eternal. Those who had grown separate from God lived lives in darkness to the light of God's loving presence, and reacted out of fear to Jesus' message and crucified him. But after three days Jesus rose from the dead, proving without a shadow of a doubt for those who saw him that life is eternal, and that the messages he taught were true. Those men who cowered at the crucifixion, now boldly praised Jesus' life and were willing to die because of their newfound conviction in eternal life, as was proved to them by Jesus.

Jesus is my Lord and Savior, for he brought me back to being aware of my oneness to God and his ever presence. I know now when I speak to Jesus, I am speaking to God. I know now that when I am speaking to God, I am speaking to myself. Does this mean that I am God complete? No. Am I a part of his creation and is he living through me? Absolutely! All I have to do is accept this awareness, and I have eternal life in this knowledge. Jesus said, "I am the way." I am now beginning to grasp these words. I am now beginning to make them mine. Thank you God. Thank you Jesus.

"The Unfinished Cross"

The work of the people of the cross is a work that is never really finished. We go about our lives doing the work of the man who died for us on a lonely, bleak hill outside Jerusalem. The meaning for our lives is tied firmly to that work.

When Jesus rose from the dead, he created a new hope, a new confidence, and a new appreciation of God with us. Not just in the moments of spiritual delight, but day by day, as we go about the work of the cross: doing good rather than evil; caring for those who most need our love; telling others of the man of the cross and what he can do in their lives, as he has done in ours.

The work of the cross is far from finished. It is a lifetime obligation for each of us. Who else can complete the work of the people of the cross except the people themselves? The power to accomplish comes from the man of the cross. The ability for others to receive the word of the cross comes from God's Spirit. But the work of the cross is ours and is a work-in-progress.

Let the unfinished cross remind you of your work, and empower you to respond to the call of God until our work together is finished. An older hymn put this question: *"Must Jesus bear the cross alone, and all the world go free? No, there's a cross for every one, and there's a cross for me."* The unfinished cross is a powerful reminder to us of the work yet to be done for Christ.

Rev. John R. Todd, Ph.D.

Author's Note About the Cover

Do you see the face of Jesus in the heart of the light? When my wife was painting several ideas for the cover of this book, she put one that was almost finished aside, and for a change of pace began on another. Although the painting she'd been working on was fairly close to being done, she wanted a break before going back to touch up a few areas.

While she continued her work, I went into her studio to see how everything was progressing. While looking at the one that was nearly finished, I did a double take and said, "Oh my God! I see the face of Jesus in your painting!" My wife stopped what she was doing and looked over to see what I was talking about, then said, "I see it too!"

Needless to say, after making this discovery she knew immediately that this was the painting we would use, and that it was finished and complete.

Her next discovery was that by moving the cross to a slightly off-center position, more depth in the colors radiated out from the light.

The face of God is everywhere. We need to just be aware and conscious of it. Even though this experience was quite startling and amazing, at some level we both knew and believed that this was possible. If God can express himself through my pen, then surely he can express himself through her paint brush.

And we have since discovered that there is even more to this painting, inasmuch as there are faces and images portraying a multi-dimensional culture of people surrounding the face of Jesus. And further still, you can see angels surrounding them as well, showing that we are all connected together and to one source, that which is simply, God.

Authentic truth—all cultures and all people connected to the source. Jesus said "I am the light." Follow the light and have eternal life in the awareness of God's great abundance.

About the Author

Born the son of one of the most decorated chaplains in the history of the U.S. Naval Chaplains Corps, Dave's father gave communion on his belly as machine gun fire flew overhead at the foot of the American flag, which had just been raised at Iwo Jima during World War II. Photographer, Joseph Rosenthal, immortalized that moment with the now famous picture of soldiers putting the flag into the ground. This became a symbol of Americans fighting and dying for freedom. As a young chaplain, Dave's father, "Hammering" Hank Austin, buried 128 marines on that hill. Dave has chosen to take a similar, but somewhat different path down the road called life. A road that eventually led him to bringing this message to you, from Jesus. A message that can bring freedom to your soul.

Dave received a Bachelor of Arts degree in both psychology, due to his interest in the human mind, and physical education, because of his love of competition and sports. After graduating from college, Dave traveled the world playing and teaching tennis, while obtaining a world-ranking on the men's professional tennis tour. His tennis career proceeded to open numerous doors for him in a most interesting journey of life experiences.

Dave's life experiences have ranged from appearing in three motion pictures and numerous TV shows and commercials, to having a "pick hit" in *Billboard* magazine for a pop record he released called "Play On." Dave has been the president of several small business corporations and has devoted much of his time to various charitable causes. He has accepted guest speaking engagements all over the world from as far away as Tashkent, Uzbekistan for the President's Cup tennis tournament. Dave is married and is the father of four boys.

Index